The Way of Conscious Eating
Mastering the Choices
You Make about Food

Not achieving is depressing

The Way of Conscious Eating
Mastering the Choices
You Make about Food

Dialogues by
Jerzy Gregorek

The Happy Body Press
Woodside, California
2014

Easy choices, difficult life.
Difficult choices, easy life.

Please direct inquiries to:

The Happy Body Press
104 Alta Mesa Rd.
Woodside, CA 94062
E-mail: thbp@thehappybody.com

Library of Congress Cataloging in Publication data: 2014919153
ISBN 9780982403891

First Edition

The Way of Conscious Eating:
Mastering the Choices You Make about Food
by Jerzy Gregorek

Cover image, "The Master Chooses," by Jerzy Gregorek

Cover and text design by Alexander Atkins Design, Inc.

Manufactured and printed in the US, on acid-free paper.

To my clients, who made me conscious of the struggle between the Fatalist and the Master, and the resulting inner dialogues

CONTENTS

PROLOGUE

A person is free if a person has a choice. But with the choice comes responsibility. I recently watched a documentary called *Fed Up*, prompting me to feel "fed up" myself, with all the films filled with blaming and complaining, ending fatalistically without a solution. What happened to Walt Whitman's saying, "Do I contradict myself? Very well, then I contradict myself. I am large. I contain multitudes." If these filmmakers contradicted themselves, then they would be able to find balance or middle ground. But their linear way of thinking prevents them from helping people to find balance because it would involve finding enough—and that is a lot more difficult than scaring people with videos of barrels of sugar, government manipulation and irresponsible advertisements that leave us with feelings of anger and fatalism. What we need is honest movies embracing contradictions. We need movies that can teach us how to fit into today's world. Teach us how to transition from less healthy food to more healthy food, if we wish. The main problem with these kinds of films is that they rely on sensationalism, for purposes of marketing what would otherwise be a boring message about the need for self-control and self-reliance. I couldn't recall how many times I have heard that sugar is added to food and that it is the main cause of obesity, causing illnesses like diabetes, while the blunt truth is that we are obese because we eat too much. We could eat French fries every day and still lose weight or not be obese, as long as we don't eat too much. Since the solution is so simple yet at the same time extremely difficult to talk about, nobody talks about it. Scaring is easy, talk is cheap and fear is convenient.

Prohibition could stop people from drinking excessively and laws can stop smokers from smoking in public places. We cannot stop people from eating or force them to eat healthy food, nor can we force them to eat less. We can, however, educate people to take better care of themselves and to make the kind of personal choices that would improve their lives.

I love potatoes—either boiled, in *pierogi* (dumplings), or as French fries—and I have learned to eat them in a way that fits my lifestyle. I also love sugar and food bars and hamburgers. I find it offensive and depressing to be told that I cannot be thin or fit unless I stop eating these foods. At one time, I was an alcoholic, after which for many years I could not eat anything to control my diet except food bars loaded with sugar. Whenever I wanted to eat bread, my body would shake. So I returned to bars, which helped me maintain my desired body weight, by satisfying my craving for sugar, thereby preventing me from overeating. Today I eat a modest portion of potatoes (baked, French fries or *pierogi*) three or four times a week, as my entire meal, and I must say that this is the cheapest lunch or dinner I can possibly have. When I go to my favorite hamburger place, I order either a protein style hamburger for $2.35 or French fries for $1.65. Once a week, I go to another hamburger joint, always ordering

French fries, with extra garlic. Delicious salsa with which I fill my plate before my fries are ready, is available there for free on the condiments bar, as are sauerkraut and jalapenos, before my fries arrive.

America is an incredible country, offering an abundance of choices and amounts, in the food that is served. When we came to this country in 1986, we had only $77 dollars to feed ourselves for a month and yet we ate like royalty. Once a week, we would go to a large market in Los Angeles, where we would buy fruits and vegetables: one dollar for five pounds of apples, grapes, oranges, beets, carrots and potatoes. Five dollars was enough to buy 25 pounds of fruits and veggies. One of our clients told us about a place in Van Nuys where we bought ten pounds of chicken legs for $3, ten pounds of rice for $2, a loaf of bread for $1.50, five pounds of ham for $3 and ten pounds of potatoes for $3. We cooked beets, carrots, broccoli and mushrooms, to make various kinds of soups. We grilled chicken and served it with veggies or potatoes or used it in soups. We made potato pancakes. We made fruit salads for desserts. We ate better than ever, healthfully and inexpensively—we just ate too much. After some months, we noticed that we had gained weight, so we spent even less money and consumed less, in order to lose excess fat.

In today's world more than ever, we need help with making intelligent decisions. Constant blaming weakens us by implanting in our brains the idea that the solution to our problems is outside of us. We have reached a point where we know what is good for us yet are powerless to make good choices. With the Fatalist in us is stronger than ever, we need help from others, in order to make better choices. We need role models for graceful living. We need to learn how to notice when others are eating too much and then how to help them. We need to learn to stop ourselves when we keep reaching again and again for more food, even though we know we have had already had enough.

It's easy to keep blaming and expecting others to solve our simple problem—eating more than we need. We do not fall into such a situation when we care about what happens to us. We care about our future but the overwhelming presence of the Fatalist does not allow us to create for ourselves a new and desirable future. With adequate practice, however, this can all be changed. We need to awaken inside of us the voice of independence and cherish the freedom of choice, becoming role models for others and for our children. We need to reach inside of ourselves and tame the voice of the Fatalist within. Without us, there can be no change and there will be more depression, because we just want to eat a little more than we need. Extending the pleasure of our palettes is more important than our well-being. If you really want to help, then show your family and friends why uprooting the Fatalist is important and why living without it is liberating.

A Plea to the Medical Community

You are the best thing that has ever happened to us. You have found cures for many diseases that previously killed millions. You have showed us the importance of better hygiene. For a century, we have gone to see you whenever we needed to deliver a baby, recover from sickness or simply felt weak and wanted to understand why. Every time, you served us with your devotion, knowledge and contemporary scientific medicine, to help us with our illnesses and conditions that worsen our health.

Having written poetry for more than thirty years, I have learned that the most difficult and moving art is about unfortunate people. Writing glorious poems about how great we are is easy but writing poems about how shameful or destructive we are is difficult. It calls for great courage and humility to share moments that have made our lives worse, in order that they can be felt but not repeated.

Humankind today is in unfortunate situation. Life today is not asking you anymore to be a scientist. It is asking you to be an artist. Our health does not get worse because we are sick or we get older. Today we become obese and develop conditions related to overeating—high blood pressure, osteoporosis, type II diabetes and others—which could easily be prevented.

We want you to keep searching for new drugs to help us with all our aliments and maybe one day to extend our lifespans even further than today. But until these drugs are available, we ask that you inspire us to eat consciously and to create for ourselves the internal drive to listen and follow the voice of the Master within us. Often you tell us to lose weight or exercise but observing you with the same unhealthy conditions discourages us, causing us to lose our struggle to achieve a healthy body weight.

We turn again to you for help. We know that it will be difficult for you to become more than you are but we do not know where else to turn. You are the vital pillar that must support our health. You have the potential to change our situations for the better and we hope that you will live up to the task.

NOT ONLY

The doctor told his patient,
"You are diabetic.
Don't wait any longer—lose weight."
"What about you?
You're obese, too."
The doctor did not say anything
but he could not stop thinking about it.
Later, he shared the story with his colleague
who told him, "I thought
you had noticed that the doctor's

calling has changed."
"So it isn't just saving lives anymore?"
"Not only that. It's even bigger.
We've become medicine itself."
"But how can a doctor heal?"
"He climbs the tallest mountain."
"But I wasn't taught that.
It's not my responsibility."
"What is,
if not
becoming healing?"

INTRODUCTION
Costly Failures, Precious Miracles

There are times in life when we feel overwhelmed and nothing seems to work. Whatever we plan requires weeks or months to achieve and we do not feel as if we have that much time. The sense of urgency in us is heightened. The thought that we need to fix the problem tells us that immediate results are needed. Planning to actually achieve the desired results becomes impossible. We begin to worry and become anxious about our future. The pursuit of anything ends up as failure. We blame our misfortune on our parents, friends, God—whomever comes to mind. We want go to sleep but we do not want to wake up.

When this feeling dominates our life, it is impossible for us to recover on our own. We need help and we are lucky when the right person appears at the right time in our life and has time to drag us off our deathbed. At such times, people who love us check us into rehab centers or similar places where we can recover in ourselves the desire to care about our life.

During my 30 years of practice, I have worked with thousands of people, about five percent of whom were in this impossible stage. They did not come to me on their own. Usually they were sent by spouses, parents or friends. When I asked them why they came, the answers were: my wife sent me, my brother sent me, my mother sent me and so on. Sometimes it was a 16-year-old boy, sometimes a 40-year-old woman or a 60-year-old man.

Despite the differences in age, there was one common belief they all shared: They were all fatalists, not caring about their lives and therefore unable to plan or follow through with plans, to simply achieve a better standard of living. As fatalists, we think that because we do not care about our lives, this does not mean that we do not care about the lives of others. We think that we own the right to not care for ourselves.

The fatalist in us deprives us of the imagination that could help us. Fatalists cannot imagine their spouses suffering, because the fatalists do not care. They do not see others as weak and sad. Their children feel abandoned and are therefore less confident. There is less focus in the family on education, on their children coming home with lower grades than before. Fatalists do not even notice when old friends avoid them. When they are at this stage, all decisions are fatalistic, only heightening their trauma. What follows is my own story, about how I became entrapped by this powerful feeling and how I was helped to recover.

I remember how when I was seven, I went with my mother to a nearby farmers market. On the way, my mother was holding my hand. I felt so happy, safe and proud to be her son—she was my whole world. At the market when we were buying eggs, a farmer asked me how old I was, to which I answered with pride that I was seven and in a month I was going to attend first grade. She smiled and said, "It's wonderful that you look forward to going to school. Do you know what you want to be when you grow up?"

I was happy when adults talked to me, so I answered

right away: "I will be a pilot." My mother looked at me with so much love that I felt as if I could really fly. When we were back at home, she said, "I am so happy you want to be a pilot but I want you to remember that you can be whatever you decide to be."

For the next eight years, my mother kept telling me that I could be whatever I want to be. The environment where I lived, however, was telling me something quite different. I lived in a community of railroad factory workers. My father was a metal worker. When I was 14 years old, he told me to enroll in a locksmith trade school, as he had. He said, "You will not only learn there but you will also be paid because you will be working three days out of five, so you will learn how to make things."

"But Dad," I said, "I want to be a pilot."

"A pilot," he laughed. "Who put such stupid ideas into your head? Pilot training school is for those who are chosen for that, not for us. We are manual laborers, workers. You will go to trade school, the same way that others from our community do, and earn money." I said nothing but when I talked to my mother, she told me to go where my heart was telling me to go. So when I finished elementary school, I applied against my father's wishes to the most prestigious high school in our town, on track to becoming a pilot. After passing the exams, I was regarded as one of the brightest kids in the city.

My father maintained his silence at all times. On September 1, I attended class at this high school for the first time. My mother was happy, although she did not express her happiness when my father was present. The first week passed very quickly. When the second week started, it revealed what was for me an unbearable truth. Almost all the other students were more advanced than I was. Their parents, most of whom had college degrees, had helped them prepare for school even before it began, while I was still partying. The gap was obvious. In the next two weeks, I was getting Cs and Fs, while almost everyone else was getting As and Bs.

I was increasingly aware of being on the receiving end of jokes. Eventually, when I could no longer bear the situation, I stopped going to the prestigious high school and signed up for trade school, to become a locksmith. Here the situation was the opposite: I was an A student, while others were getting Fs. But that didn't make me feel better. I knew that there were others, elsewhere, much better than I, which made me increasingly depressed.

When we got paid at the end of a month, I would go with others for a drink, usually beer or wine. As the months went by, I was drinking more and more—until six months later, I was expelled from school. Thus began my life as an alcoholic. Every day, I would leave the house and meet with others like me. Together, we foraged for money to buy beer, wine or vodka. At the end of the day, I would come home drunk. I would wake up the next morning without remembering half of the previous day.

Sometimes I lost two or three days in a row, leaving home on a Friday and coming back on a Monday, thinking it was a Saturday. Thoughts of despair became more frequent and pronounced but I did not have the strength to stop them. I felt as if I was having an out-of-body experience, watching things from a distance.

One day three years later, I went to a party where I met some of my old weightlifting friends. One of them shared his story about his father throwing all of his weightlifting equipment out of the house. "I need to train but I have nowhere to go," Mirek said.

To which I responded, "You can come to my place."

"Really?" Mirek replied happily.

"Sure," I said.

What he didn't know was that, as an alcoholic, my enthusiasm was not grounded in reality. I had a very short-term perspective and I didn't remember my promises.

The next afternoon, I was napping while drunk, when I heard a loud knock on my window. I hobbled over to the window, where I saw Mirek, standing there with all his weightlifting equipment.

"What are you doing here?" I asked.

"You told me yesterday that I could bring my stuff over and we could train together."

"Well, if I said so, than come in and have fun, while I continue my nap." Of course, I didn't remember what I had promised him the day before.

After Mirek brought all his equipment into my room, he set up a bench. "Come on, let's do something together," he offered.

"Forget it," I barked.

But Mirek wouldn't give up easily. After several more attempts, he uttered the magic words: "OK, let's just do a few presses together and then we'll go for a beer, on me."

My ears perked up when I heard the word beer. I rolled over on the bed, now facing him. Mirek was sitting on the bench. All the weights were neatly placed against the wall. He looked happy. There was something very appealing about him. It was a feeling I remembered but could not pinpoint.

"Just a light workout for ten minutes and then we'll go."

"OK," I said, pulling myself out of bed.

"Lie on the bench and I'll give you the bar."

The bar felt very heavy to me after I grabbed it. I couldn't do a single press.

"Let me spot you," Mirek said, while he grabbed the bar and helped me press it several times. I felt the warmth in his voice when he spoke.

After we finished, we went for beer to a bar where we encountered some friends. We drank, talked and laughed together. After two beers, I could no longer walk straight.

"That's enough for today," Mirek said. "Let's meet again tomorrow and have some more beers." He and his friends walked me back home.

The next day when I was napping, Mirek came back and the day repeated itself. As the weeks passed, our trainings together became longer—15 minutes, 30 minutes, one hour, two hours.

After six months, I was a lot stronger. I hadn't really noticed that I was hanging out more with Mirek and his friend than with my alcoholic friends. After a year, I was as strong as Mirek. We now trained together twice daily and drank only occasionally. My mother was happy. She liked Mirek and all his friends.

I was now sober. I didn't really know how it happened. I started having conversations with neighbors and friends that I had not spoken with for many years. A new world was opening up to me, a completely new world. It was as if I had been born again.

In the spring of 1974, I began working as a fireman. That summer, I went through intensive preparation for re-entry into the high school that I had left in shame. After my application was accepted, I was overjoyed. Soon thereafter, I was confronted with an overwhelming reality. My friends who had started the same year I had were already in their second year in universities, studying to become doctors, lawyers, engineers and so on.

On the first day of school, Mirek sat together with me when the teacher welcomed and introduced everyone. I was both happy and ashamed but this time I was able to bury my shame deep inside of myself and keep studying. This time, I studied constantly and everywhere—like a mad man, greedy for knowledge: in school, in the fire department, at home, during walks, as we trained. I used every available second to catch up. Only two years earlier, I had been sleeping sometimes beside the curb, as the rainwater from the gutter washed over me, rousing me from my drunken stupor. "Hey, look, that's Jerzy," I sometimes overheard passersby saying. "What a shame. He had so much talent."

In May 1975, I finished the first year with an award. With pride, I walked over to meet Aniela, who was at the time my girlfriend, and showed her the prize, a book. In her happiness, I felt again the same warmth as I had felt from my mother and from Mirek. I also started to feel it more often, from teachers and new friends.

I had been fortunate. My alcoholic friend Jasiu, who was one year older than I, had died when he was 21. During the next few years, others had followed him.

HOPE

My Russian teacher shouted,
"Jura! You will never learn a second
language." I sat with my eyes cast down,
my cheeks burning.
After the class some students
talked to me, but I couldn't
understand them. Never,
never, never swelled in my head
like spoiled fish in a can.

I started meeting Jasiu more often.
He always kept
a bottle of wine for me.
We drank until Never

waved like worms down my body
and squeezed itself
into the cobblestones.

The last time I saw Jasiu,
he was asleep,
hugging a 12-gallon jug,
a tube in his mouth,
wine still dripping
to the cement cellar floor.

The next day, I found his last
bottle of wine and the note,
"Always yours, Jasiu."
When we buried him,
we noticed how light his coffin was, but
but still we almost dropped it,
shaking on our soft legs.

How did it happen that I was spared? I had been
blessed, by people who supported me, by being there for
me—by their special kind of energy. They helped me to
move through the day with less darkness each time, until
a beam of light finally ignited in me, the light I still carry
today, a light of constant desire to improve myself and
others, circumstances notwithstanding.

I am sure you also remember a feeling inside you,
telling you that everything was good in your life. You
wake up and you are excited about the day. In the past,

you made creative decisions and you took appropriate actions to achieve your goals. Nothing that needs to be done overwhelms you, regardless of whether it requires weeks or months or even a lifetime to achieve the goals that you are ready to pursue. All strategies appear in your mind as if they were heaven sent. Planning meals and following the plan is not only easy—it is exhilarating. You cannot wait to wake up at 6 am and exercise or meditate or do whatever is necessary to improve your or someone else's life. The future is exciting and it promises even more growth. You feel good and you are happy.

Of course, there are not many moments like that in life and there are not many people who can be at this stage for a prolonged period of time but I have been blessed to know some of them.

In October 1981, I was studying engineering at the Fire Protection Academy in Warsaw. It was my last year and I was getting ready to start a new chapter in life together with my wife. The following July, I was to be sent somewhere in Poland to serve as an officer fireman. This meant that I might be living in a city I had never been to before. It also meant that I would get an apartment—a dream for young people like my wife and me. To have an apartment in Poland was almost impossible but in only eight months, we were to be in our own new apartment. I would have a good salary and it would be a perfect time to start our family. I received a list of options from which I was able to request my preferences. I preferred to be in Warsaw, where I would be able to pursue studies in chemistry, eventually earning a Ph.D.

Before coming to the Academy, I had served for five years in the fire department. My five-year delay had provided me with a wealth of experience. Usually the boys that came to the Academy came directly from high school. I, on the other hand, came with five years of experience in the fire department and the rank of senior corporal. Because of my age and my experience, I was voted leader of my class. The second year, I was elected student leader of the entire school. With my master's thesis almost completed, I was poised to begin to enjoy the fruits of my labors.

Enveloped in my dreams, I floated through the Academy as if on a flying carpet. But as my mother used to say, "Don't be so happy today—because then you will be unhappy tomorrow." It was time for events in my life to take a sharp turn. It was 1981 in Poland, at the time of the Solidarity movement. Everyone was at the same time both excited and scared. People became kind to each other, generating a feeling that the whole country was turning into one beautiful and omnipotent entity. The feeling of togetherness and courage was being awakened throughout the country.

Poland was becoming a war zone without war. Demonstrations were occurring everywhere. Thousands of people no longer scared poured out of their homes to tell the communist government, "Enough!" Hundreds of people were being arrested daily. That is when I received important news from two members of the Solidarity movement who were teachers at the Academy: Alina

Dobrowolska, who taught computer science, and Marek Surala, who taught physics. At a secret meeting, they informed me that General Wojciech Jaruzelski, whom the Russians had made president of Poland, had a plan to utilize the Academy for the purpose of defeating Solidarity. The idea was to change the status of the Academy from a public to a paramilitary organization. This would have enabled Jaruzelski to utilize the fire department to quell demonstrations.

I had a very uneasy feeling inside, a feeling that I was about to lose everything I had worked toward, both professionally and personally. But the alternative, of not doing anything to oppose this plan, was even worse. "What can we do?" I asked.

"I don't know," Marek said.

"I don't know if you are willing to risk your position but in my opinion, you should tell all the students the truth," Alina said.

"You know what will happen if I do that. I will be blacklisted."

"It's your call," Marek added. "Whatever you do is up to you. We fulfilled our responsibility and now it is time for you to fulfill yours."

"Okay," I said. "I will talk to the heads of each year's class and will see what they want to do."

After a short discussion, all student leaders decided to inform all the students about the situation. At the meeting, some four hundred student firemen decided to initiate a peaceful protest. Even though the protest was innocent, it disturbed many officers whose responsibility was to keep the students uninformed and pacified. But the officers were losing their grip over the students from the first and second years who lived on the Academy campus.

When the officers fired shots at 10 pm on November 25 in 1981, I ordered an emergency meeting of all students. The third and fourth year students lived one hour from the Academy. When we arrived, the gate was locked. We were unable to enter the building without assistance. We asked Solidarity members to help us. After about an hour, Marek Holuszko, together with some workers from the Warsaw Steel factory, came to help by supporting and by witnessing the present situation, to prevent violence from breaking out.

Seeing the overwhelming support received from Solidarity members, the officers on duty opened the gate of the Academy, allowing us to gather in the main lecture hall. After an hour, all students voted in favor of an occupied strike and I announced that the strike had begun.

The next day, no one could enter the building. All teachers and staff stood outside. The police arrived, as did more Solidarity members. Police set up a fence around the building, preventing anyone from entering. Thousands of people, including students' parents, came to support us, with food and moral support. At the end of the day, it was clear to everyone that we would not back down unless the school was allowed to maintain its status as a strictly civilian organization.

Negotiations began with the government. To help us deal with an increasingly intense situation, three particular individuals came to help. Seweryn Jaworski, who represented Solidarity, ensured direct communication with Solidarity headquarters in Warsaw. Kazimierz Wejchert, a professor at Warsaw Polytechnic University, helped us formulate our demands in correct legal language. Jerzy Popieluszko, a priest, came from the Church of St. Kostki to offer us moral and spiritual support.

When Wejchert and Jaworski came, it was obvious to me that they had one purpose: the establishment of a free and independent Poland. I was extremely impressed with these two men and did everything I could to be around them and learn as much as I could from them.

At first, I could not imagine that anyone could be more inspiring than these two men but I was wrong. Jerzy Popieluszko was even more amazing. He had a calm and loving presence, emanating peacefulness, free of aggressiveness or anxiety. In his presence, my fears and worries about the future dissipated. I was 27 at that time and it was the first time I encountered someone who loved me unconditionally. No matter how my disbelief tried to discredit the possibility of being loved simply because I was a human being, it could not succeed. For the next ten days and nights, I lived on coffee and cigarettes, without sleeping. Unfortunately, after ten days of negotiations, the Polish government decided to end our strike by force. Police stormed the building from the ground, while a special antiterrorist brigade used helicopters to land on the roof. They found four hundred of us gathered in the main hall, after which they announced that the academy no longer existed. We were ordered to leave the building. We were also presented with an option to swear allegiance to the new school, if we wanted to continue our studies.

THE LAST FIRE

"Government gives Fire Academy to the army,"
the broadcast said while I was cleaning a ladder;
I sat down and held my head between my hands
covered with ashes from last night's fire.

I was one semester
from graduating to fulfill
my childhood dream—I was five
the first time I ran out of the house
after hearing a fire siren.
Without waving my hands,
I stood still at the curb looking
at the passing truck—I wanted to be
inside a fireman's uniform,
to become a friend of fires,
to crawl between flames.

But the broadcast meant
I would have to color water
to spray Solidarity demonstrators
so they could be recognized and arrested.

We marched by the hundreds
to the lecture hall
and raised our fists,
"NO!"

The next day, policemen surrounded the school
while our families, steel factory workers,
and professors stood behind them in the snow,
trying to pass
a cigarette, an apple.

Each evening we prayed with Popieluszko,
the patron of the Warsaw Steel Factory,
who filled us with enough courage
to close our eyes at night.

On the tenth morning,
pieces from broken doors burst
ahead of policemen who kicked us
till they'd warmed their cold feet.

We were given one chance to swear
allegiance to the new school
governed by Jaruzelski's comrades.
We didn't even consider it—
they loaded us into buses
and drove away between soldiers
gathered around tanks.

But we weren't scared,
we just looked behind them
to where our empty fire engines
stood in the garage.

Sometimes, today, even in my forties
I want to jump onto
a passing fire truck, tie my
uniform whose sleeves still smell
of the last fire around my sweaty skin,
but instead I stand with my eyes
on the line of the horizon
where I saw the last blue light
flashing—the sound of a siren still
caressing my dry ears.

Even though I loved being a fireman, I decided
together with more than a hundred others not to swear
allegiance to a new Fire Protection Academy, focusing on
helping other students to get into different schools and
find them support while they studied. My underground
experience began in Jerzy Popieluszko's church. To be
close to Jerzy was a blessing. Whenever I met him, I felt
as if I got a shot of love. Millions of other Poles felt the
same way. Jerzy's sermons became increasingly powerful
because of their power of love. Unfortunately, the leaders
of the Polish government could not stand it anymore.
On October 19, 1984, four policemen kidnaped Jerzy,
tortured him and threw his body into a river.

EVEN IN THE ICY RIVER

Every morning I walked into the church
where Jerzy Popieluszko,
the Warsaw Steel Factory priest,
prayed with the workers.
Usually, at the beginning of a sermon,
he lifted his eyelids and kept looking
until the silence brought us back from yesterday.
Then he covered his hollowed cheeks
with his long fingers and began,
"Love. Open our fists."

He traveled from one church to another
but one day in the early morning
four policemen stopped his car.
They threw his body into the trunk and
and drove to the nearby forest
where they hit him
with metal clubs, screaming,
"Open our fists,
open our fists!
Where is your love?"

They couldn't see that he had already left,
that he kept his head down praying for them
even when they tightened a rope
around his feet and attached rocks,
even when they cut his stomach,
and even when they threw his body into the icy river.
The river we drink water from.

The loss to the Polish people was overwhelming. I fell into a deep depression and could not come out of it. Spending weeks in the church did not help. In February 1985, I was still depressed, so when I was ordered to come for an interrogation to the police station in Szczecin, I did not care if anything happened to me. The next day at the police station, I was sent to a big room to wait my turn. There were maybe fifty other people waiting, as I sat on a bench and began reading a book. After several minutes, a man came into the room. I recognized my close friend Mietek, from the Szczecin Olympic Weightlifting team. Together with Otto and Wojtek, Mietek and I were close friends, always training together and having fun. I rushed over to him and shook his hand. We were happy for a moment, the intervening years seemingly irrelevant. He was the first to break our joy. "What are you doing here?" he asked.

I told him my story about studying fire protection engineering.

Then I asked him, "What have you been doing?" He looked at me with a strange kind of gaze I had never seen before, one that made me feel uncomfortable.

"No," I said.

"Yes," he said, "I became an officer a some years ago." Then he added, "Let me find out what is going on with you." He took my paper and went through a nearby door. After a few minutes, he returned with my paper. "It's not good. I was able to cover up for you. Don't come back here ever again. If you do, you will never leave."

"Are you sure about that?" I asked.

"Yes," he said. "I am sure. You had been assigned to me."

"So that means ... ?" I stopped myself, before completing the sentence. Mietek was silent.

I shook his hand and said, "What a life this is, eh?"

When I told my wife the story, she said, "It's clear that you have to leave the country now. I will stay behind, so they don't suspect that you are escaping."

I left Poland as soon as I was able to obtain a passport, a few weeks later, on March 8, International Women's Day, probably the happiest day in Poland. On this day, all women are showered with flowers and gifts. Everyone is friendly with each other, even when they are not acquainted, and everyone nurtures one another.

I said goodbye to Aniela that day, without knowing when we would see each other again. In Sweden, I immediately checked into the Solidarity headquarters in Stockholm, where I learned that my depression was minor in comparison with others. People like I were separated from their loved ones. Husbands waited for years for their wives and children to join them but the Polish government would not release them, suspecting the whole family would stay abroad permanently. Keeping families apart was a form of punishment.

Usually situations like these ended in hunger strikes. Sometimes a man whose family was still in Poland would sit in front of the Polish Embassy for days without food and would eventually be reunited with his family. Sometimes he would be taken to a hospital because of weakness and exhaustion.

The suffering of Polish people in Stockholm moved

me and inspired to help. Instead of complaining about my own situation, I began helping others by supporting them with inspiring words. As I talked with people, I began to experience a feeling similar to when I was traveling in a fire truck to a fire scene for the first time. I felt proud that someone somewhere needed me and I was going to help. More and more people came to my place and asked me to help them sort things out.

People started calling me a village priest, which could not have made me happier. One day, a psychologist from Poland named Wanda Saj came to me for help. After several meetings, she said, "You have a certain clarity when you talk. I don't know how to describe it but it is very helpful. I encourage you strongly to write."

"Write?" I asked. "Why should I write?"

"Because you have something to offer and you should care enough to pass it along to others."

I was speechless. My mind was racing. In Poland, I was always a scientist and never an artist. All books that I had ever read were about science.

Wanda patiently awaited my answer.

"But I have never written anything," I said. "How could I write without having learned how?"

"It's not important how you write. What's important is that you do it," she said, with a pleasant smile.

"Okay," I said, "I will try."

"Don't try," she said. "Just do it. Write."

It was almost midnight when I came back to my hotel room. I sat at my desk, took out a pen and stared at a blank page. No thoughts came to me. Nothing important was happening in my head. I closed my eyes and spent about twenty minutes sitting silently. My whole life was rolling in front of me as if I was in a movie theater.

When it ended, I opened my eyes and wrote the first word: "Rebirth." Then I started writing sentences. After writing two sentences, it became clear that I was writing a poem, even though I had never read one in my entire life. I thought for a moment that this may be temporary but as I turned the page and kept writing, it continued to be verse.

When I met Wanda the next day, I gave her the poem. She looked at it, then at me and back at the poem, after which she said, "I knew that there was something about you that I couldn't grasp, but now I see it. You are a poet."

I laughed and said, "Just writing a poem does not make me a poet. To be a poet, one needs to have a life calling for this."

"You will have such a calling. I'm sure about that."

"Well, I don't know about that. There are more important things on my mind right now than writing poetry."

"You will do important things and you will also write poetry. About this, I am certain. I feel it. And I think that you should stay in Sweden and we should open a practice together, so you can continue helping people."

I liked Wanda and I didn't know how to tell her that I was not going to stay but it seemed she already knew.

"You intend to leave, right?"

"Yes, I have to," I said.

"Why? Sweden is a beautiful country. There are many people that need your gift and you will have plenty of time to write poetry."

"You see," I said, "when I was 15, someone asked me where I was born, meaning where in Poland. But when I wanted to answer, I had a feeling that I didn't really belong there." At that point, I wondered whether I should continue.

"You can tell me," Wanda said, reassuringly. "Everything is safe with me." Wanda had a very inviting and harmless nature. I trusted her.

"Well, my body was born in Poland but my mind ...." I hesitated for a moment. Without knowing why, I said, "But I feel as if my mind was not born in Poland."

Wanda was looking deep inside me and said, "In America, right?"

I was surprised. "How did you know?" I have seen it before. I hoped that maybe you could find a home here but you have to liberate yourself and become independent before you will find peace and devote yourself to a higher purpose."

I didn't understand what she meant by a higher purpose but I was glad she agreed with my calling.

I was able to leave Sweden faster than I thought I would be able to. Within a week, I received a phone call from the CIA office in Munich, Germany. The Warsaw underground, especially people that were involved in the strike and Radio Solidarity, experienced many arrests. I was called to Munich to help identify the spy within the underground, the person responsible for the arrests.

During the next three weeks at the CIA office in Munich, I revealed what I knew, hoping that this would contribute to identifying the spy within the movement. Shortly afterward, my wife and I were granted status as political refugees in the US. With a $1,000 in savings and one huge piece of luggage, we landed at JFK Airport in New York. We then boarded another plane for Detroit, where our sponsoring company was located.

Although we made it to our destination, our luggage unfortunately did not. It was somehow lost, never to be found. Aniela looked very upset, so I told her that maybe God wants us to discard everything from the old country and begin a completely new life here. This at least seemed to offer her a certain degree of comfort, seeing how calm I was.

During our stay in Germany, we had befriended Andrzej, who was now in Los Angeles and offered help if we wanted to relocate there. In the morning, we said goodbye to our sponsors in Detroit and took a taxi to the airport. The tickets to LA cost us $400, leaving us with only $600 and the clothes on our backs. As our plane approached Los Angeles at 11 pm, the city was illuminated below us. It was magical to see so many lights. Even pools were lit. I was mesmerized by the beauty and the power.

Aniela looked worried, so I said, "In two years, we will have a house with a pool, too." That was a mistake. Aniela looked at me as if I had lost my mind. Years later, she admitted that she really thought so. For the next two weeks, we were preoccupied with survival. We slept on the floor in different homes almost every day. Later, a kind Polish family who lived in Los Feliz let us sleep in the unfinished second house they were building. It was cold but it was where we found our first home in America. We warmed each other under three blankets and dreamed about having our own place.

After two weeks, I was rejected for employment by a fire department. I was told that, at 32, I was too old and over qualified, in terms of both education and experience. A month passed and I still could not find a job. With the idea of utilizing my expertise as an Olympic weightlifting coach, I made an appointment with Bob Hise, president of the AWA (American Weightlifting Association) and went to see him in Eagle Rock. Bob was a great man. People loved him and obviously respected him. I told him who I was and asked about any opportunity to make a living doing training for Olympic Weightlifting. "There is no money in weightlifting," he said. "All coaches who come from Eastern Block countries open auto repair or body shops and make a very good living at it. If you want to fix cars I can introduce you to some of them."

"I don't want to fix cars," I said.

Bob thought for a moment and said, "There's a new trend in gyms with something called personal trainers, which is something you could try. But Olympic weight-lifting coaches don't like to work with regular people, so I don't know if you would like that but you could try."

"Where could I find such a gym?" I asked.

"I don't know," Bob said, "but you could look around and eventually find one. You don't need a car."

My wife and I walked in increasingly larger circles from where we were staying in Los Feliz. One day, we arrived at a place called Power Source in Burbank. After I introduced myself to Aram, the owner, I asked about the possibility of working in the gym as a personal trainer.

"The best I could do for you is to hire you for a one-week trial period. I would pay you $5 an hour and you would work five hours a day, for five days." Aram shook my hand and wished me luck.

"But what exactly should I do?" I asked. Aram smiled and said, "I really don't know. You'll have to figure that out as you go. You have a week to make it work."

Aniela was happy. "You got a job!" she said, hugging me. "But you will need gym shoes," she added. We found the nearest Salvation Army outlet and walked inside. The only gym shoes that fit me cost a dollar but they happened to be pink. I bought them. The next day, in my bright pink shoes, I stood in the gym, ready for my new career. Jimmy, a manger, knew about me and greeted me with a big smile that got even broader after he saw my shoes.

"What should I do?" I asked.

"Well," Jimmy said, "If someone new comes to the gym, he will get a free session with you and your job will be to help him become familiar with the gym equipment. If he has any questions about health or fitness, you will do your best to help him.

"If he likes what you've done for him, he may want some private sessions with you. If a person buys a session, he will pay us $25, of which 60 percent will be yours."

I immediately calculated that I could earn $15 an hour, which was a lot of money for me at the time. The first person who was referred to me reported back pains and said he wanted to lose weight. I created a daily routine for him, to make his back more flexible and I designed a food plan so he could lose weight.

The next person referred to me had high cholesterol and high blood pressure. I also created for her a specific exercise routine and a food plan. The next referral was a model who wanted a more attractive and agile body. I also designed a plan for her to follow so she could achieve her goals.

After a few hours, there were no new referrals, so I looked around the gym for anyone who looked if he or she needed help. In the far corner of the gym, I spotted two men in their early 30s doing deadlifts. They were both about 6-foot-4 and 300 pounds. Both of them were lifting 315 pounds. It was obvious to me that although they were big, they were weak for their size and had very poor lifting technique, which would prevent them from getting stronger. They rounded their backs, to compensate for their weak leg muscles. If they continued this way, they would end up with stronger backs but even weaker legs, which would eventually lead to herniated discs.

I walked directly over to them to tell them. They stared down at my five-foot, six-inch frame, weighing only 130 pounds and wearing pink shoes. I felt that if I didn't do something dramatic, they would grab me by my shirt and carry me out of the gym. So I walked over to the bar that was loaded with 315 pounds and said, "Here: Let me show you."

Surprised and amused, they decided to watch and see what would happen. The weight was heavy even for them and of course they couldn't imagine that I could lift it off the ground. I grabbed the bar and lifted it six times, in rapid succession, about one second for each rep. After I set the bar down, I said, "If you lift like this instead, your legs will get stronger and you'll avoid injuring your back."

They just stood there, dumbfounded, without saying anything. In the absence of any response, I walked over to the reception area, to see whether there were any new referrals for me.

The next day, the two men approached me to thank me and to shake my hand. I later learned that they were both night club bouncers. Years later, this connection came in handy, as they introduced us to other bouncers, who spared us from waiting in long lines.

The news about my ability to enable people to become stronger, lose weight or get off medications spread quickly throughout the gym and beyond. New people coming to the gym were asking specifically for me. I was soon working fourteen hours a day, seven days a week. Almost overnight, I lost my fear of not having enough money. My wife had a very similar experience.

We worked, worked and worked. Two years passed by very quickly. One day, a client of ours named Karl Angel asked me whether I go out. "Go out?" I asked. "What do you mean by that?"

"I mean go out for dinner?"

"No," I said. "We have never been out for dinner here. We eat at home."

"Well," he said, "let me introduce you to a great place. It's Italian and the restaurant has been operated by the same family for three generations."

"No," I said. "We do not want to go."

Karl looked at me and said, "Come on, let me take you there. It will be fun."

For some reason, I didn't want to disappoint him, so I agreed.

Saturday evening, dressed as if were going to a wedding, we were picked up by Karl and his wife, Lisset.

The restaurant was great. All the food looked fantastic and was delicious. It was the first time that I had gnocchi. I always liked anything cooked with potatoes and my mother cooked a very similar dish, called kopytka. This was our first time in an American restaurant and when time came to pay, Karl—who knew how hard we worked and how difficult it was for us to live—tried to prepare me for his paying for our dinner. Of course he knew how that could be difficult because I took pride in being independent. So when he offered to pay for us I said absolutely not. He made a couple more attempts but finally gave up after it was apparent that I would not accept.

This experience had a big effect on us. We realized that people here have a different approach to life and it would be good for us to go out sometimes. So whenever we had time, we would go out for breakfast together and we enjoyed being served.

Food was sometimes a topic of conversation when I trained my clients, so when Thomas Griffith found out that we had never eaten sushi, he insisted on inviting us to his favorite sushi bar. This time it was easier for me to agree. The next day, he and his wife, Mary, picked us up and took us to the restaurant. Of course, they ordered everything and the first thing I tasted was white tuna albacore. Thomas and Mary watched when I put the piece of sushi into my mouth. It was soft, warm and very tasty. My expression when swallowing prompted them to shout, "Yes, yes!" My wife loved sushi, too, and we ate a lot that day. When the time came to pay, Thomas said, "Let me treat you guys. It would be my pleasure." This time it was easy for me to simply say thank you. Slowly, we were becoming Americans, working hard and enjoying our lives.

In 1989, everybody talked about houses, the values of which were increasing virtually overnight. It seemed that if we didn't buy right away, we would never be able to afford a home. We didn't have enough money for a down payment but some of our clients offered to pay us in advance for six months of services.

Karl helped us find a real estate agent and we were ready to find our first home. When I talked to my client Pat Wallace about our intention, she suggested that we rent rather than buy. "Houses are now overpriced," she said. "They will decline in value within a year or two. Why not wait a while? Save up some more money and you will have your house soon."

But the prospect of having our own home in combination with other people's anxiety about this was keeping us up at night. Our emotions and imagination were driving us to buy, in spite of some warning signs that the time was not right.

Our agent found us a home in Van Nuys, a three-bedroom fixer upper with a pool. My dream was coming true. The house was listed for $220,000 and when we asked our agent how we should proceed, she said that we should offer full price if we like the home and want to buy it, even though it needed a lot of work. In six weeks, escrow closed and we had the keys in our hands, as we walked with our client Chris Huntley for the first time into our new home.

When I opened the door, I was reminded that it smelled terribly and it was dirty. Everything from the roof to the floor had to be replaced. When we were outside after seeing everything, I said, "Well, in a month, we will have a big party." Both Aniela and Chris looked at me as if I had lost my mind. Indeed, it took us a whole year and about $40,000 to fix it but it certainly looked beautiful—white with black trim and a red door— dressed in bougainvillea, above the front entrance.

Our housewarming party was a blast. Probably two hundred people showed up and brought all kind of things we needed for our house, as well as all the food for the potluck. We enjoyed the house immensely, inviting many of our clients, who became our friends. Life became stable and we saw the promise of a great future ahead of us.

Even though we could not imagine that anything bad would happen to us, the depression of 1990 came, bringing with it the collapse of real estate values. Almost overnight, our home's value dropped 50 percent, to $110,000. For the next few years, we concentrated on working and paying the bills. After five years, however, the negative situation began to take its toll on us.

We visited our bank to propose to sell the house based on the current market value. But the bank representative told us that this is not the way business is done in America and if we wanted to keep the house, we needed to continue to make our payments. I suggested that if the house was foreclosed on, the bank would probably lose even more money but that didn't change anything. The banker simply answered that if they allowed us to do that, everyone else would want to lower their payments and the lender would lose too much money.

Drained by the whole situation, we decided to let the house go into foreclosure, even though some of our clients suggested that we rent it out and wait for values to come back. We thought about it but we didn't have the energy for that and chose instead to return to apartment living, as tenants. So it was that we moved from Van Nuys to an apartment in Marina Del Rey.

We needed new purpose and motivation, to find meaning in life after losing everything that we had worked for during the past ten years. Back to where we had started a decade ago, we tried to comprehend what had just happened. The only solution seemed to be to move forward.

Our desire for emotional and spiritual recovery prompted us to enter the MFA program in creative writing at Vermont College, with an emphasis in poetry. We also started competing in Masters Weightlifting championships and we formed an Olympic Weightlifting Team at Gold's Gym in Venice, California. School, competition, work and coaching took our minds off of thinking about the past, about thinking of losing our home and our sense of security.

We graduated in 1998 with MFA degrees in creative writing. Two years earlier, we had competed in the 1996 World Weightlifting championship in Canada, with Aniela wining gold and me silver. We competed in Poland at the weightlifting championship in 1997, wining two gold medals. In 1998, because I was injured, I did not enter the Nike World Masters Games. Aniela did and won the games. In 1999, we went to Scotland, where we both won the Masters World Weightlifting championship. That year, we moved our team to UCLA and founded the UCLA weightlifting team, registering it with United States Weightlifting Federation in Colorado Springs. Some members of the team entered the State Weightlifting Championship in 2004. Walter Chi won state championship and Michael Casey came in third.

Two thousand four was another year of great change for us. After 25 years, we were blessed with a pregnancy, with Aniela expecting in August. Michelle and David Kelly, who were moving to Woodside, told us that it would be a wonderful place to raise our child. We drove there the next weekend, to have a look. As soon as we drove into the village, we were in love with Woodside.

We could not afford to live there, however, unless we could borrow money toward a down payment for a new home. With Aniela five months pregnant, we relived the scenario from 15 years before, putting together a down payment with the help of our clients, who advanced us six months of fees for services. We made the purchase in June and moved in on the Fourth of July, at 2 am.

Natalie was born on August 16 and I was working very hard again to pay our bills. Most of our clients were in Los Angeles, so for the next two years, we drove to Los Angeles every Friday, after seeing clients in Woodside, to spend the weekend in Southern California. Aniela, Natalie and I were staying at a Studio City guesthouse that two of our clients, Madeleine and Jeffrey Tucker, were kind enough to let us use. We would see some of our clients at the guesthouse, while we would drive to the homes of others.

On Monday, I would coach the UCLA weightlifting team until 11:30 am, after which we would drive back to Woodside, where I would see my first client there at 5:30 pm. Week after week for the next two years, this was our life. Our fear of failure gradually diminished, as our client roster in Woodside steadily grew. During drive time, we wrote *The Happy Body* book, which was published in 2009. The next five years were concentrated on helping people achieve *The Happy Body* lifestyle.

I noticed that even though people knew what was good for them and had plans and a strategy to achieve it, they would easily jeopardize their efforts by following destructive habits. It became clear to me that people need inspiration. Whenever someone allowed the voice of the Fatalist to dominate, it would destroy what the individual wanted to create. I wrote a poem to help them to identify not with the voice of the Fatalist but with that of the Master, who is able to do what we often do not like but is nonetheless good for us. After five years, I had written 56 poems, which I later published under the title, *A Healthy Mirror for Change: Nourishing an Appetite for Losing Weight*. These poems proved very helpful in fighting destructive decisions.

During the past year, I realized that my clients were expressing themselves in strongly contradictory voices. Just five minutes after committing to losing weight, someone would say that it would be impossible. I began identifying internal dialogues that go on within us. In so doing, I helped my clients to see that we are not destined to a certain way of living, that how we live is the result of our decisions. I learned that there is a constant dialogue within us and that dialogue is between two opposing forces: the Fatalist and the Master. The one that dominates shapes our life.

As I explored the language of these two dominant forces within us, I increasingly came to the realization that there is a natural tendency to identify with the Master (a heroic, positive force) and turn away from the Fatalist. Even if initially only for a moment, this energy accumulates over time to the point that it eventually begins to effect a transformation, by means of internal dialogue.

As I watched people change in their orientation from Fatalist to Master, I noticed changes in the way they use language. In the first week of practicing *The Happy Body*, practitioners report choosing the wrong foods or food amounts, without any real awareness of doing it, as if their knowledge of what was right was suspended during the time that the transgressions are committed. People on the program who are unable to lose weight become disappointed, frustrated and unhappy.

When they are in the second week of the program, they report being aware of choosing the wrong foods but they feel as if they are watching the scenario from the outside, rather than exercising control over what happens. During this phase, certain individuals are still unable to lose weight, even though they experience a weak positive voice that gives them hope.

In the third week, they report having an internal debate that could sometimes go on for minutes, before either the Fatalist or Master within them prevails. One day, it might be the Fatalist within them that prevails. Another day, it may be the Master. The situation is fluid, capable of changing within minutes. People in this phase could follow the program perfectly for three days—and then fail for two—or any combination (3-4, 5-2, 7-3 or whatever). They usually lose three pounds and gain the weight back or they sometimes go on like this, back and forth, for months. They lose 30 or 40 pounds over time and then gain them back, obliged to begin anew.

The fourth week is usually a breakthrough. People still have an internal conversation but this time the Master within them is much stronger in terms of contributing to the decision. At this point, practitioners know that they are improving and happy to share this with others. They are still afraid of gaining weight, although the voice of the Fatalist at this time is weak, without the power to prompt the individual to regain weight. Upon entering my studio, these people are beaming with pride and happiness. They know they are changing for the better and that nothing threatens this progress.

In the fifth week, practitioners stop experiencing the negative voice of the Fatalist altogether. All decisions are positive and constructive. As they no longer need my services with regard to weight loss, I ask them to become more independent, coming only occasionally or whenever they really need supplemental information relating to the program.

As I analyzed my clients' situations in terms of failures relating to losing weight, thereby becoming disappointed and unhappy, I identified 12 common challenging situations. I then wrote five-level dialogues between Fatalist and Master, in response to these situations.

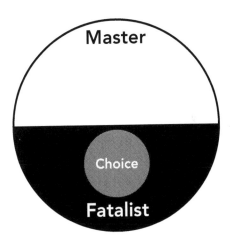

The first level, which I call Fatalist, is dominated completely by the voice of the Fatalist. A person in this situation needs outside help because there is no help offered by the Master, who is entirely absent from the internal dialogue. When I was an alcoholic, I could not pull myself out of the addiction without outside help from Mirek. On a daily basis, Mirek channeled the voice of the Master for me.

In my thirties, when I ate food from a plate or bowl or pot, I would keep eating until I finished everything, even if my stomach hurt. On one occasion, Aniela videotaped me. A fruit salad was left after a party we gave. The contents of the large wooden bowl easily exceeded ten pounds. I sat outside, with the bowl between my legs, as I began eating. When I watched the video, I noticed that I didn't take my gaze off the contents of the bowl, even for a second. It was only after I had finished that I lifted my head, at which time I saw Aniela filming. She laughed as if she had been watching an entertaining comedy. This was the first time that I consciously became aware of my eating habit.

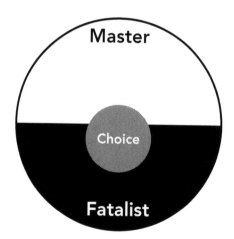

The second level, which I refer to as the Disbeliever, represents the relative strength of Fatalist as 75% and the Master as 25%. A person at this level cannot make a positive choice even though it is provided. When I was buying a home, Pat was the voice of the Master, showing me the best choice for me at the time. I was blinded, however, by the voice within me of the Fatalist, who was impatient and could not wait. When we lived in Marina Del Rey, we had a weekly all-you-can-eat Sunday buffet brunch at The Warehouse Restaurant on Admiralty Way. We usually arrived before 10 am, the first diners to enter. There were tables outside with a clear view of water and sailboats. It was beautiful. We sat there and usually enjoyed the scenery for a while, as we drank champagne. Then we began our trips to the inside where we found the food: steak, potatoes, fish, pork chops, mushrooms and so on. Stomach pains usually began after an hour, with the Master within us suggesting that we either pause or stop eating altogether, as we had already gotten our money's worth. But the voice of the Fatalist was too strong. We just kept on eating, finishing three hours later, at 1 pm, with coffee and the last piece of my favorite, tiramisu cake. We lived close by, so in five minutes, we were back in our apartment. After another five minutes, we fell into a sleeping stupor, snoring for another several hours. We would usually wake up at 5 pm, groggy and surprised by where the day had gone.

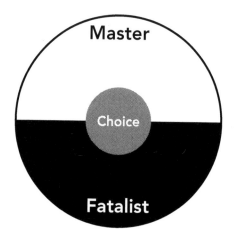

The third level, which I call the Debater, happens when the Fatalist and the Master carry equal influence. At this level, it is difficult to make a decision. Usually we struggle until we are tired and our willpower is weak, at which the outcome can go either way.

In 2002, we lived in Santa Monica, where we loved to go for dinner to a friend's restaurant, La Vecchia Cucina. There they baked a delicious, crispy homemade Panini bread. The bread would come out steaming hot from the oven, after which it was offered with olive oil, basil and garlic, which we would scoop up in large quantities using the bread. Usually before we ate anything else, we had two or three loaves of Panini bread, by which time we were full. But we ordered food anyway, so as not to offend the waiter.

One day, Aniela suggested we go there but I refused. "The bread is too powerful. If I go there, I will come back seven pounds heavier."

Aniela shrugged her shoulders. "Okay," she said. "We can always stay home and make dinner ourselves." She went to the kitchen and started looking for ingredients.

I went to the office and paced like a tiger, back and forth, as my internal dialogue proceeded: "I love the restaurant but I cannot go there. This is ridiculous. I must go and conquer the bread. It is either me or the bread that will emerge the winner. Today, I will conquer the bread. I cannot allow the bread to be stronger than I am. How is it possible that bread could be stronger than a poet, a teacher, a world weightlifting champion?"

So we decided to go. When I entered the restaurant, I seated myself immediately at the bar. Mark the bartender usually worked on Friday evenings and gave us our customary drinks. Without any hesitation, he poured my favorite drink, vodka with fresh lime. I called this drink a foggy. As Mark brought out the bread with olive oil and extra basil and garlic, I was just finishing my drink. I put the glass down and asked Mark to refill it. Then, with one hand, I grabbed one piece of bread and inhaled its fragrance deeply. With the other hand, I held my hand with the bread, preventing myself from putting the bread into my mouth. It was difficult but it worked.

With my second drink, I repeated the action with the bread. This time, it was much easier to resist. The third time, I just smelled it—without holding my arm, as I had seen Russian weightlifters do—and put it back. I don't know what happened with my brain but the bread had lost its power over me and the game was over. We returned to this restaurant many times, without stuffing ourselves with the bread. The Master within me had triumphed.

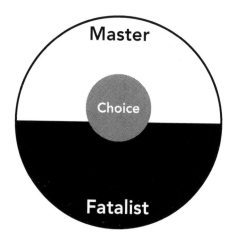

The fourth level, which I have named the Hesitator, represents the strength of the Fatalist at 25% and the Master at 75%. A person on this level makes a positive choice even though the voice of the Fatalist tries to dissuade against making the right choice. When Michelle and David told us that Woodside would be a great place for our daughter, Natalie, to grow up, we made the decision to move there even though our entire clientele was located in the Los Angeles area, where many friends also lived. In short, we loved the area and felt it would be a tremendous sacrifice to leave but the welfare of our child was more important.

In 1997, four days before leaving for Scotland to compete in the Masters World Weightlifting championship, Marek and Malgosia Probosz celebrated Marek's birthday and invited us to the party. We adored them but with only four days before the competition, any intake of excess food would put us at risk of weighing too much and therefore dehydrating our bodies just hours before competition, thereby running the risk of becoming too weak and forfeiting our chance of winning. When I told Aniela that we could attend the party, she said: "Of course we can go. We have to go and be able to have fun with these guys, as we do the right thing for ourselves. We need to learn to cope with such challenges."

I wanted to go, so I said: "Okay, let's go."

Aware of our situation, Malgosia and Marek didn't expect us. So when we showed up, they were extremely happy. The voices of our Masters within us were strong. We ate only what we needed, as we engaged in conversation and dancing. We hadn't even noticed that five hours had passed and it was time to go home.

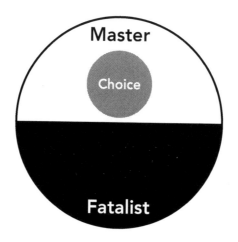

The fifth and last level, which I call the Master, is dominated 100% by the voice of the Master. At this level, we don't make any negative or destructive decisions. As my body ages and my metabolic rate drops, my body requires less food, so I simply adapt to the amount my body needs. In so doing, I avoid all the disappointment, frustration and suffering involved with gaining excess weight.

After living for sixty years, I have learned that most of our decisions are about simple things we do on a daily basis like eating a bagel or drinking a glass of juice, going to a movie or staying home. These decisions are so rooted in the past that it is impossible for us to change anything unless we change our past. We eat more then we need to because that's what we did in the past. We spend hours each day on the Internet because that's what we have done in the past. There are other decisions that can affect our lives negatively.

Had I not left Poland, would I still be alive? This is something I will never know. Some decisions, on the other hand, have definite negative repercussions. The pain of loss with which they are associated makes it difficult to forget these things. After we lost our home, whenever I dwelled on it, I became depressed. Even today, after many years have passed, I still think about what might have been if I hadn't bought the home that I lost or if I had bought it after the economic downturn, for $110,000, instead of the $220,000 I had paid for it before the crash. My life would be so less painful and I would not have found myself fifteen years later in the same position, without a home, borrowing money to buy another dream home.

We tend to make choices based on our past, with intuition developed from past experiences. But in order to make the decisions that are best for ourselves, we must break free of the past. Since we cling to our past—and all the choices we make are based on our intuition—we are unable to create a better past for ourselves. We need to be aware of our situation and choose what our past does not like but it is good for us. We must make conscious choices until they become our past and our intuition develops from this "new" past.

This book will enable you, first, to identify the voices of the Fatalist and the Master within you. Second, it will help you to become conscious about the voices, by writing your own dialogues. Third, it will empower you with ability to apply what you have learned in actual situations, observing not only the Fatalist and Master within you but also within others.

How to Use This Book

This book was written to make your life better, by making you aware of the different voices that speak within you while dealing with food. First, you will become aware that you have voices, so you will not have to depend anymore on believing in destiny. As soon as you become aware of these voices, you will start to recognize them in the dialogues. Second, after you are able to recognize the voices, you will start practicing to write your own dialogues. After practicing all the dialogues, you will gain the ability to realize that any situation creates a power struggle within us and that you will be able to direct this struggle to the constructive outcome by leaning toward the Master. As soon as you gain this ability to choose the Master within you, you will be able to recognize the voices outside of yourself—in your friends family members, as well as strangers—and you will be able to help them to become aware and guide them to work with themselves to achieve this life-changing power, reflected in the voice of the Master.

First, read the dialogues and become aware of your inner dialogues. Second, practice writing all the dialogues provided in Part II: Practice Writing Dialogues. Third, after you have developed the ability to write out all these dialogues, start applying them to real life. Go for example to a dinner with friends and listen to your inner voices, as well as to those of others. As soon as you are able to consciously recognize all the different voices within you and within others, you will become liberated from both the Fatalist within you and the Fatalist in others.

For ease of reading, the voice of the (slanted, distorted) Fatalist is represented in italics, while that of the (upright, balanced) Master is non-italicized.

Part I
Identify the Voices Within

THE SCALE

Scenario 1. Jen is standing on the scale, which shows a three-pound gain from the day before.

I. Fatalist:

"I messed up again.
What was I thinking?
It's not normal at my age to be thin.
Once again, I fell into the trap
of vanity and anti-aging.
How foolish I am."

II. Disbeliever:

"I messed up again.
What was I thinking?
It's not normal at my age to be thin.
Once again, I fell into the trap
of vanity and anti-aging.
How foolish I am."

"You can always start again.
You know better than I
that the past is not interesting.
We only change in the present.
So try to focus on the choices
you're making right now."

"It's too hard, and I don't even know
if what I want is possible.
It seems that I want to buy the dream
of being young, when I'm already old."

"But you're only 47.
That's not old, and being healthy is not
vanity. I'm sure that if you think about
your health, things will improve."

"That's easier said than done.
I'm always tired, and it makes me feel old.
I don't even have the energy
to think about cooking healthy meals
or doing the right kind of exercise."

"I'm sure you still have the energy
you had when you built your business."

"Maybe. Although all I want to do nowadays is sleep."

III. Debater:

"I messed up again.
What was I thinking?
It's not normal at my age to be thin.
Once again, I fell into the trap
of vanity and anti-aging.
How foolish I am."

"A trap? What are you talking about?
Wanting to be healthy is not a trap.
It's normal at your age to want
to be healthy and youthful,
and, most of all, attractive."

*"But I'm tired all the time, and I hurt —
my knee hurts, my shoulder hurts,
and everything else feels this way, too.
I can barely walk upstairs,
and you expect me to run on a treadmill?"*

"I know it may sound strange, but exercise
is not as important for losing weight as people think it is.
But I know for sure that when you lose weight,
you will have more energy and be able to
run up those stairs effortlessly."

*"Are you crazy? Exercise is everything.
Look at those people who are old and thin.
They work out at least two hours a day.
If I tried that, I'd be in a hospital
after just three days."*

"I know that's how it seems,
but many people who live to be more than a hundred
are thin and don't exercise at all."

"You must be kidding."

"I never kid. You know that.
The research is clear."

"*Really? Well, I once read that
you can eat more and lose weight, too.*"

"Well, then, let's do our own research."

IV. Hesitator:

"I messed up again at the party yesterday.
Next time, I'll need a plan to stop myself from eating
nuts.
I only gained three pounds, which I'm sure
is all water, because of the salt and sugar."

"*I've heard that many times before.
You say that every time you come back from a party.
Maybe it's time to be okay with getting old.*"

"I'm okay with getting old, but I'm not okay
with being weak and in pain."

"*Isn't that normal at your age?*"

"No. If there's even one person my age who feels better
than I do, it's enough for me to want to feel better, too.
I'll come up with a plan right now."

V. Master:

"Well, the scale doesn't lie. I knew
I'd gain this weight, and I did.
But, it's amazing how easy it is to actually lose weight
when I follow my plan."

BREAKFAST

Scenario 2. It is 7AM. Jen is staring at a piece of bread with a thin layer of almond butter on top of it. Her nutritionist told her the day before to consume no more than 150 calories for breakfast in order to lose 45 pounds of fat in seven months.

I. Fatalist:

"This piece of bread looks ridiculous.
I'll die if I eat so little.
He must have lost his mind.
I have to report him to the Better Business Bureau
and find somebody more reasonable.
Meantime, I'll have some bacon and sausages
to be sure I get enough nutrition."

II. Disbeliever:

"This piece of bread looks ridiculous.
I'll die if I eat so little.
He must have lost his mind.
I have to report him to the Better Business Bureau
and find somebody more reasonable.
Meantime, I'll have some bacon and sausages
to be sure I get enough nutrition."

"Yes, the bread may look small,
but what if it's enough for you?
Adam has helped many people
so he probably wouldn't make a mistake."

*"I'm sure he didn't make a mistake
because he is either crazy or he hates me.
If I eat only this piece of bread
and walk to work, I could pass out
while crossing the street."*

"That's not going to happen.
You have lots of food already stored in your body
and it's available all the time.

*"You never know.
Are you willing to guarantee I won't drop dead?"*

"Well, I'm sure you won't drop dead,
but I can't guarantee it."

*"See? It's easy to suggest, but not so easy
to stand behind your suggestions."*

"It's not about that. It's just that nobody
can ever guarantee that another person will live."

*"I see that you're very confused, so let's just say
it's enough and enjoy the right breakfast."*

"But."

"I said enough. You'll never enjoy life
if you deprive yourself."

III. Debater:

"This piece of bread looks ridiculous.
I'll die if I eat so little.
He must have lost his mind.
I have to report him to the Better Business Bureau
and find somebody more reasonable.
Meantime, I'll have some bacon and sausages
to be sure I get enough nutrition."

"The piece of bread is enough for you to lose weight.
You've probably forgotten that you saw a nutritionist
just yesterday who prescribed a program to help you
lose forty-five pounds of fat in seven months."

"I don't think he had any idea about my appetite."

"Appetite has nothing to do with weight loss.
It's time for you to become a scientist when it comes to food.
Your body wants to eat more and your mind wants to eat more,
so you need something to trust that tells you how much is enough."

"I think that a body is more complex than science.
We still don't know many things about our body.
I would not trust science about food. It's because of science
we produce food that can trigger cancer and other deadly conditions."

"It's true what you say, but would you agree that a person has
to consume more than a person needs in order to gain weight,
and that a person has to eat less then a person needs
in order to lose weight?
And that this simple knowledge could help
when we want to change our weight?"

*"It's clear to me, but I cannot imagine
that a piece of bread is enough for my breakfast.
It must have no more than 150 calories."*

"Let me help you with this.
Adam said that you need 300 calories
but if you take in only 150, the other 150 calories
will come from the fat your body already has.
You'll still have the right number of calories. Be satisfied
and you will lose all the fat you want."

"That would be great, but I still do not believe that it's possible."

"What if you test it? Follow the program for a week
and if you do not lose weight I will be quiet,
but if you lose, you will continue."

"OK, I can do that as a test."

"Deal?"

"Deal."

IV. Hesitator:

"It's amazing that this piece of bread is enough for my breakfast.
What could I have been feeding in the past?"

*"I wouldn't be so fast to accept such a small amount of food.
If you deprive yourself, you can get sick.
I would go to a doctor to check it out."*

"I don't think I need a doctor to tell me
that losing forty-five pounds is good for me.
Actually, I'm sure that it would make my doctor happy.
He's been nagging me to lose weight for the last ten years."

*"But what if you don't know when to stop?
You could end up getting sick."*

"I read that I should weigh about 150 pounds
and I researched top athletes and found out
that most of them are just about that weight.

"Look. I just don't want you to get hurt. That's all."

V. Master:

"How liberating it is to know that
one piece of bread is enough.
Science can help us to improve, after all.
I'm blessed that I found out how to use it
on my own behalf."

LUNCH

Scenario 3. Jen is sitting with three friends at a table in a restaurant, reading the menu.

Jen's friend, Angela, always had a perfect body. June is 20–30 pounds overweight and has always struggled with losing weight. Monica, who is about 100 pounds overweight, has never seemed to care about her weight problem.

I. Fatalist:

"This restaurant is fantastic.
I'm glad Monica chose it.
I will have a cheeseburger,
fries, and a milk shake.
Poor Angela. She will have
salad and tea. June will
usually start with a diet Coke
and end up with fifteen French fries.
And Monica will have what I have.
She is always happy and
agrees with whatever anyone wants.
She's always so pleasant to be around."

II. Disbeliever:

"This restaurant is fantastic.

I'm glad Monica chose it.
I will have a cheeseburger,
fries, and a milk shake.
Poor Angela. She will have
salad and tea. June will
usually start with a diet Coke
and end up with fifteen French fries.
And Monica will have what I have.
She is always happy and
agrees with whatever anyone wants.
She's always so pleasant to be around."

"But you ate a turkey sandwich only two hours ago.
Maybe you could have some salad to help
digest all this bread and meat?"

"Oh, you want me to be like June,
desiring something I can't get."

"But I'm sure you can be like Angela.
It's just that you have to eat less and make better choices."

"The problem is that I don't want to be like
Angela or June, but like Monica.
Look at her—she knows how to live.
Always happy and pleasant to anyone."

"But it ..."

"Oh, stop whining."

III. Debater:

"This restaurant is fantastic.
I'm glad Monica chose it.
I will have a cheeseburger,
fries, and a milk shake.
Poor Angela. She will have
salad and tea. June will
usually start with a diet Coke
and end up with fifteen French fries.
And Monica will have what I have.
She is always happy and
agrees with whatever anyone wants.
She's always so pleasant to be around."

"You must be completely lost."
"Oh, no, let's have a salad and tea."

"You must be kidding. I would starve."

"Starve! You just probably ate a thousand
calories in one sandwich. If anything
would starve, it would be your mind."

"You don't understand hunger.
Every cell of my body is screaming
for food and if I don't eat, I'm sure I will die."

"So how do you explain gaining five pounds
every month."

*"It's simple. It's hormonal. Every month
I have a period. Got that?"*

"So why were you fifty pounds lighter a year ago?"

"OK. What if I add a salad to my order?"

"That's even worse. You need to compromise.
What if you eat fries and a salad?"

"You must be kidding."

"What about a cheeseburger and a salad?"

"And a milk shake?"

"No."

"No way."

"OK. What about a milk shake and a salad?"

"But that's not a dinner at all."

"You have to compromise. It's either
fries and a salad, burger and a salad, shake and a salad,
or no dinner at all."

*"Well, let me think. What is the biggest?
I will have a cheeseburger, but no salad.
I don't want Monica to see my weakness."*

84

"Fine."

IV. Hesitator:

"This restaurant is difficult.
Of course Monica chose it.
It will be difficult to order anything healthy here.
I wonder what Angela will order.
Perhaps, as usual, just a salad and tea.

"But I heard it's a great restaurant.
They have healthy hamburgers from grass-fed cows,
they use organically grown potatoes for fries,
and their milk comes from
free-range, grass-fed cows as well. Maybe
a hamburger would be great today.
You didn't have a hamburger for more
than a month and you're hungry."

"You're right. I don't even remember when I last ate a hamburger,
but I don't want to be unhealthy anymore and look like
Monica.
I will have a salad and tea."

"You're not fun anymore."

"That's OK. I will find fun another way."

V. Master:

"This restaurant is horrible.
Only hamburgers and fries.
There is only one person who could choose this place.
I will have a salad and tea."

DOCTOR'S OFFICE

Scenario 4. Jen's doctor tells her, "You're are already pre-diabetic. With your family history, if you don't lose at least 25 pounds in a hurry, you could become diabetic within six months."

I. Fatalist:

"He must be kidding. I'll bet
he didn't look in the mirror for quite a while.
He's probably fatter than I am.
How dare he tell someone else to lose weight?"

II. Disbeliever:

"He must be kidding. I'll bet
he didn't look in the mirror for quite a while.
He's probably fatter than I am.
How dare he tell someone else to lose weight?"

"He's a doctor.
I'm sure he's right about losing weight.
He must know what he's doing."

"He's supposed to be a good example
to inspire people and not weaken them.
But, look at him."

"That doesn't excuse you from getting healthier."

"I don't know anymore who is healthier.
If he's a doctor and he doesn't know, then who does?"

III. Debater:

"He must be kidding. I'll bet
he didn't look in the mirror for quite a while.
He's probably fatter than I am.
How dare he tell someone else to lose weight?"

"Who cares that he's overweight.
You're the one in danger. Why don't you just focus on that?"

"If I'm in danger, then he is too.
Should I tell him that?"

"You still don't get it, do you? You just look
for one excuse after another, so you don't have to lose weight."

"No, no. I just don't have any interest in losing weight."

"Okay then. What if you change doctors?"

"I don't want to change doctors.
He's kind and always polite.

I would miss him."

"Then why you don't agree with what he says?
It shouldn't be that difficult to lose some weight."

*"What if I come back to see him in three months?
Maybe he exaggerates because he doesn't want
to be responsible in case something happens."*

"Are you crazy?
You're pre-diabetic and if you get diabetes
your life will be miserable.
Don't you care?"

"Three months is not going make that much of a difference."

"What about a month?"

"Let's make it six weeks."

"Great."

IV. Hesitator:

"How did it happen? I have to lose this fat.
Tomorrow I'll see a nutritionist."

*"Wait, wait. What's the rush?
It's not like your doctor is any lighter than you*

and he doesn't have a problem."

"I don't care whether he has a problem.
I'm scared. I want to get better now."

"But maybe he's wrong."

"Well, losing some weight shouldn't be
harmful. Don't you think so?"

"I just don't want to rush. That's all."

V. Master:

"I'll start today.
Diabetes is nasty.
It's only twenty-five pounds of fat.
I can lose that in four months."

INSIDE THE GROCERY STORE

Scenario 5. Jen walked into the grocery store from the side where fruits and vegetables are displayed.

I. Fatalist:

"It's amazing that people still
have to cook when there are
so many wonderful products ready
to heat up and be eaten in minutes.
I guess people are still poor.
Well, I'm not poor,
so I'll go to the middle section
and buy some frozen packages
for breakfasts, lunches, and dinners.
It's so wonderful to be rich."

II. Disbeliever:

"It's amazing that people still
have to cook when there are
so many wonderful products ready
to heat up and be eaten in minutes.
I guess people are still poor.
Well, I'm not poor,
so I'll go to the middle section
and buy some frozen packages

for breakfasts, lunches, and dinners.
It's so wonderful to be rich."

"Having delicious food ready
to eat in minutes is fantastic,
but maybe sometimes we should
cook food to make a special dinner?"

"You can't be serious. Only poor people
cook today. I don't want to send the wrong message
to my children. They're still very fragile
and can easily adopt bad habits."

"I don't think that children would be hurt
by preparing fresh food. People today say
that making food at home can actually be
healthier than eating food that is preserved."

"If you keep listening to people who are
as poor as vegetables in the store
you will end up begging on the street."

"I just somehow like the look of fresh
vegetables and fruit, especially their colors."

"I hope it is just an artistic attraction,
otherwise I would worry."

III. Debater:

"It's amazing that people still
have to cook when there are
so many wonderful products ready
to heat up and be eaten in minutes.
I guess people are still poor.
Well, I'm not poor,
so I'll go to the middle section
and buy some frozen packages
for breakfasts, lunches, and dinners.
It's so wonderful to be rich."

"Come on, let's buy some fruit and vegetables.
They are healthy and can help to fight aging."

"And who will cook? Did you forget
you don't even know how to boil potatoes?"

"I'm not stupid. I'll learn. There are many books
and there are also many wonderful cooking classes
at the store and in schools."

"You will learn? You must be kidding.
After thirty years of living, you don't even know
how to peel potatoes and clean and prepare a chicken."

"I said I would learn and I will.
It can be a bonding experience for everyone.
Once a week, we could all plan

to cook a meal
we would enjoy eating."

"*Maybe you will, although I doubt it.
Besides, I don't want children to bond while cooking.
I think it's better for it to happen while eating.
I have the best conversations while sitting
at a dinner table where our food is served.*"

"It's just about having a hands-on experience."

"*What if one of them meets a cook and wants to marry him?*"

"Why not?"

"*Have you lost your mind, or forgotten
that we don't mingle with workers?*"

"Well, I would hope it's time."

"*Not while I'm alive.*"

"Well then, let's make a fruit salad tonight."

"*But we will buy fruit that's already prepared.*"

"Of course."

IV. Hesitator:

"We're so blessed to have stores
full of colorful and nutritious produce.
I can cook fresh and different dishes every day.
Staying healthy is so easy and so gratifying.
Nothing is better than touching vegetables,
cutting them, cooking your own meal, and enjoying
their aromas as they fill the home."

*"You know, sometimes we don't have the time,
so maybe you can pick up some frozen packages, just in case."*

"It's sad that a person doesn't have time to prepare
her own meal, and by the way, would you like to eat food
that may have been prepared last year or even two years ago?

V. Master:

"My goodness! I have never seen so many fresh vegetables here.
This grocery store is getting better and better.
I think I'll buy more vegetables and invite my neighbor friend
over for a meal. She said she finds cooking such a bore.
Hopefully she will accept, and I'll be able to teach her
how to cook from scratch."

THE LAST 10 POUNDS

Scenario 6. Jen is reading a chart that shows no weight loss during the past two years, even though she tried everything to achieve her goal.

I. Fatalist:

"You just don't get it!
Weighing the same as
when you were a teen
isn't natural, it's unhealthy.
You are like Sisyphus who
tries to lose the last ten pounds
that can never be lost.
Just enjoy being the way you are.
Life is short. There's no time for heroes."

II. Disbeliever:

"You just don't get it!
Weighing the same as
when you were a teen
isn't natural, it's unhealthy.
You are like Sisyphus who
tries to lose the last ten pounds
that can never be lost.
Just enjoy being the way you are.
Life is short. There's no time for heroes."

"I agree that life is short.
But I also worry that I can make it shorter.
Maybe we didn't find the right way.
It shouldn't be so difficult to lose some weight."

"We spent two years trying,
and I don't want to live
in a dream anymore. There's nothing
wrong with being a little plump."

"It's really not only about health.
I'm still young and I don't want to live
just a mediocre life.

"You'll get used to being ordinary.
Everybody does."

III. Debater:

"You just don't get it!
Weighing the same as
when you were a teen
isn't natural, it's unhealthy.
You are like Sisyphus who
tries to lose the last ten pounds
that can never be lost.
Just enjoy being the way you are.
Life is short. There's no time for heroes."

"You want me to be Sisyphus
and you do everything to make sure I am.
As soon as I lose three pounds
you tell me to reward myself.
I don't know how I will become
conscious enough to stop
eating more than I need,
but I'm sure I will one day."

"You've been saying this for years.
Be honest with yourself.
How many times have you used fear or fantasy
to make promises to yourself?
Didn't you fly to Hawaii to learn another
special and magical program to become thin?
I feel really sorry for you."

"But I know people who were able to achieve it,
so I know I can do it, too. I know it's hard,
but what is the use of doing what is easy?
Any monkey can do that.
I want to live a youthful life and if it takes
years to create it, that's what I will do.
I don't want to waste the years I have to live anymore."

"All these people you talk about depend on being thin,
and they have strong motivations.
They are actors, models, personal trainers. It's their job.
Did you forget that you are just a housewife with three kids?"

"So, it's even more important for me to gain control
over my emotions, so my children learn
that unnecessary suffering is the product
of a weak mind, but we have a choice."

*"Well, so far you're a fake, living a life
that someday, maybe, will happen."*

"I guess you don't get it that
because our past wants us
to stay the same, for a while
we have to pretend we are already are
who we want to be.

*"So now you've become a philosopher
trying to convince yourself
that pursing the impossible makes it possible.
What a joke."*

"Your fatalist attitude only makes me
stronger. You will be surprised this year."

"I can't wait."

"Me too."

IV. Hesitater:

"It's amazing how this journey teaches me
how little food I really need to live a great life.
I'll even spend less money than last year.
If I'd only known for the last ten years
how little food I really needed
I could have bought a new house."

*"Too little food can be fatal, so I would eat
a little more in case you miss some nutrients."*

"I don't have to worry about that,
after all, I'm still carrying a lot of fat on myself."

*"Well, it isn't about the number of calories.
The food that is produced today isn't as nutritious
as it used to be, so we eat more food to get enough nutrition."*

"Don't worry. I guess you forgot that I eat
lots of vegetables, fruits, fish and meat.
I'm sure these power foods supply the nutrients I need,
especially since they are organic."

*"I don't want you to get sick.
It's better to be safe than sorry."*

"I can always add more vegetables."

V. Master:

"My intuition deceived me again.
My past is too strong to depend on it for change.
Starting today, I'll only trust the numbers.
I will eat every three hours, five times a day,
and if I don't lose a pound a week, I will eat less.
Math is a great helper when nothing else works."

TASTING FOOD

Scenario 7. Jen has been stopped in the grocery store by a food company representative to taste a new product sample. Looking at it, she doesn't know what it is.

I. Fatalist:

"This food smells and looks so good.
I'm so happy I came today.
But the samples are so small
I will have to try two or three
to be sure, so I know this product
in case I want to buy it."

II. Disbeliever

"This food smells and looks so good.
I'm so happy I came today.
But the samples are so small
I will have to try two or three
to be sure, so I know this product
in case I want to buy it."

"But there are already more than twenty packages
of food in your refrigerator,
and there is no room for more.

Shouldn't you wait until you eat
some of what you already have?"

"*I want new food. Isn't that why I work,*
to enjoy new and delicious foods?
It's my time, and I earned the money."

III. Debater:

"*This food smells and looks so good.*
I'm so happy I came today.
But the samples are so small
I will have to try two or three
to be sure, so I know this product
in case I want to buy it."

"Don't even think about touching it."

"*Really! Don't you want to enjoy a better life?*"

"You call it a better life,
but this food looks like any other food.
There is nothing better about it.
If you they didn't tell you its name,
you wouldn't know what it was even after eating it."

"*Don't you trust your own taste?*"

"Yes, but do you really trust people
who made this yellow mass? It could
contain the worst possible ingredients?"

*"I'm sorry if you have problems with your imagination,
but I understand. Distrust has big eyes."*

"So, what would you think of yourself
knowing you had eaten
a shapeless mass of food
that might have been prepared
in a windowless basement
and in a different century?"

*"You're really getting worse.
How about getting some help?"*

"I need help? I'm the one who wants to eat fresh broccoli,
peaches, and salmon, rather this awful pile of who knows what?"

*"Then why bother with cooking
all these foods separately
when it all ends up in the stomach anyway?
Isn't 'baby food' the best?"*

"Not if you don't know what's inside.
It can be the worst.
Did you forget about throwing up on Monday?"

"You can get sick by eating spinach too, you know?"

"What if I cook tonight and you relax
by listening to your favorite music
until dinner?"

*"Now you are trying to seduce me.
I didn't know you had fallen so low."*

"What was I thinking?
I didn't realize you were so suspicious."

"So, let's taste it then."

"What if we finish the shopping first
and then come back for a taste?
Then, if we decide to buy it
we will know how much to buy."

"Are you trying to trick me?"

"Oh no, how could I?"

IV. Hesitator:

"How can people eat something
when they don't know what it is?"

"Maybe it's just about the taste.
Anyway, look at the faces
of the people tasting it.
They love it."

"I used to have the same reaction
until I read about food.
Thank God, now I know better!"

"Well, what about reading about this food?"

"Oh, my salivating friend,
one day you will stop, too."

"Can't I just taste it one last time?"

"If I allow you to do that,
it will call you again and again.
If I don't, you will forget
about this in ten minutes.
Let's go and buy some fresh broccoli."

V. Master:

"How do I get to the produce section?"

PREPARING A DINNER

Scenario 8. Jen is preparing a dinner for her friends, Anna and Fred. Fred is gluten intolerant.

I. Fatalist:

*"It's impossible to prepare
an interesting dinner without gluten.
I'm sure Fred comes from a weak family
and is faking intolerance to attract
attention. The whole dinner
will be about babying an old man.
I wish I could cancel it."*

II. Disbeliever:

*"It's impossible to prepare
an interesting dinner without gluten.
I'm sure Fred comes from a weak family
and is faking intolerance to attract
attention. The whole dinner
will be about babying an old man.
I wish I could cancel it."*

"Why would he do such a terrible thing?
He seems to be an honest and kind person."

"*I know Fred, and I'm sure he
is faking the problem to give me a hard time.*"

"Aren't you going a little to far with your accusations?"

"*Maybe he is intolerant just for the fun of it.
He can't stand watching others enjoying all the food.
Once at a wedding, I saw him leave
everything on his plate as he projected
his dissatisfied cow's eyes on everyone there.*"

"Maybe he just didn't like the food."

"*It was a wedding.
Even a fully-fed person would eat something
to share out of happiness
for the bride and groom.*"

III. Debater:

"*It's impossible to prepare
an interesting dinner without gluten.
I'm sure Fred comes from a weak family
and is faking intolerance to attract
attention. The whole dinner
will be about babying an old man.
I wish I could cancel it.*"

"He is gluten intolerant and you should be
honored to cook for him because he doesn't
allow many people to do that.
I don't know why, but he trusts you."

"If he really knew me, he would never ask me to cook for him."

"I don't understand how you
came to that insight?"

*"Come on. It's simple.
He would know I love gluten
and cannot imagine happiness without it."*

"But he wants to be happy, and
he trusts that you can surpass that weakness in yourself."

"What are you talking about? What weakness?"

"Never mind. Can't you just be more accepting?"

"Aren't you talking about pleasing?"

"Well, you aren't happy, so maybe if you
change your mind about Fred, it will help you
to see that he suffers because of this limitation."

*"Who says I'm not happy? I'm very happy,
but if somebody doesn't like the food I make, it bothers me."*

"Exactly."

"Exactly what?"

"Never mind. Keep cooking
and be proud of serving food even though
people cannot eat it."

"It's not like that. I just know that he is lying."

"That's a pretty serious thing to say. What if he doesn't lie?"

*"He won't die, and then we'll find out
whether he's lying."*

"And what will you do if...?"

"Enough."

"Do you really want to take such a risk?
How about this time you just make an exception?"

"Okay. I will compromise but only this time."

"Sure."

IV. Hesitator:

"I'm so happy I cook for Anna and Fred,
especially since Fred is gluten intolerant.
It's an opportunity for me to show them
that I care and am able to adapt to challenging situations."

"It'll be lots of work, and maybe he is just capricious.
He's always demanding and attracts lots of attention
with his outrageous needs. Do you remember last year
he became vegan because God appeared to him in a dream?"

"Maybe you're right, but I'd rather
stay in the kitchen for another hour to cook
than face the embarrassment of being insensitive."

"Come on, everyone knows that you are super sensitive,
so there's no way you could be accused of insensitivity."

"I don't want to take that risk."

V. Master:

"There's only one hour before I see Anna and Fred.
It's still enough time to prepare a dessert.
I'll make gluten-free apple pie especially for Fred
and another with gluten in case Anna
would prefer the old-fashioned kind. It'll be a wonderful evening."

"ALL YOU CAN EAT"

Scenario 9. Jen is on a ski vacation. She is in the restaurant together with her spouse and two children. She sits down at a table with three other couples and their children. There are 16 of them altogether.

The waiter presents the options: "Every Saturday, we have a special dinner, which you can order from the menu. Or you can select the all-you-can-eat buffet."

I. Fatalist:

"I'm always hungry after a dinner out
and pay too much for just a little food.
Oh, I'm so happy they have the buffet.
I look forward to recurring trips
and ever-changing food on my plate.
I feel so hungry today
I could break my record of seven plates."

II. Disbeliever:

"I'm always hungry after a dinner out
and pay too much for just a little food.
Oh, I'm so happy they have the buffet.
I look forward to recurring trips
and ever-changing food on my plate.

I feel so hungry today
I could break my record of seven plates."

"But what about all these people sitting
on the other side of the table?
They'll see how much you eat
and you know better than I
it's not a pretty picture."

"Who cares what others think.
I'm not responsible for their jealousy.
After all, thank God, we live in a free country."

III. Debater:

"I'm always hungry after a dinner out
and pay too much for just a little food.
Oh, I'm so happy they have the buffet.
I look forward to recurring trips
and ever-changing food on my plate.
I feel so hungry today
I could break my record of seven plates."

"Have you forgotten the last time
when you ate a buffer dinner?
Two families left the table
after your second plate of
mashed potatoes and sausages.

116

They felt so disgusted that they refused
to have a dinner with you since that time."

"I didn't care about them even before
so I was glad they stopped bothering me.
To tell you the truth I don't want to be
with people who don't accept me as I am."

"I understand that but you also
show children that overeating is okay
and that worries the parents who don't want
to see their children becoming obese and sick."

"As usual, you try to make me responsible
for others. I told you it's free country
and everyone should look
no farther than their own plate."

"I just worry that soon we won't have any friends."

"Who needs them, anyway?"

"Come on. You know that it isn't true. Okay?

"Okay."

"Okay."

IV. Hesitator:

"The buffet would be fantastic, but I don't
want people I don't know to see me
devouring mountains of food.
I'll order fish and asparagus though
dinner is never enough for my mind.
But it is more than enough for my body,
which I rarely experience since I eat
as if I was competing with everyone else
for an Olympic gold medal."

*"I don't understand why you're so concern about
what people say or think.
Isn't it their problem? And by their responses
they only show how prejudiced they are.
By the way, you're the fastest eater
I've ever seen. Maybe you should
enter a competition—winning could be
a turning point away from pleasing."*

"Well, if I didn't see the faces of people
with open mouths watching me pushing
a whole sausage into my mouth,
maybe I would think about competition
but I saw them and they haunt me in my dreams."

V. Master:

"Thank God they offer a dinner as well;
otherwise, I'd be stuck with the buffet
like the last time when almost everyone left the table
as I brought over my second plate.
Today, I'll follow my friend's advice
to eat as if I was a princess."

AFTER DINNER

Scenario 10. It is 7 pm. Finishing dinner, Jen has a strong urge for something sweet.

I. Fatalist:

"The dinner was so delicious,
but I need something sweet
to make it even more special.
I will have vanilla ice cream
topped with caramel and chocolate
and, of course, some cookies for crunching."

II. Disbeliever:

"The dinner was so delicious,
but I need something sweet
to make it even more special.
I will have vanilla ice cream
topped with caramel and chocolate
and, of course, some cookies for crunching."

"You just had dinner and you're probably full.
Don't you think it would be better to wait
an hour or two until the food is digested?
The ice cream will taste better if you do."

"You know that if I wait one hour
I'll eat the whole quart, but if I eat
right now I will be satisfied with
just three scoops."

"I remember last week after a dinner
you went for a walk and then
went right to bed
without eating ice cream at all."

"That's exactly why I can't go for a walk.
I don't want to forget my ice cream.
In fact, it's time to swallow that heavenly food."

"But it's just food."

"You don't know what heaven is
so stop talking and enjoy
the river of joy sliding down your throat."

III. Debater:

"The dinner was so delicious,
but I need something sweet
to make it even more special.
I will have vanilla ice cream
topped with caramel and chocolate
and, of course, some cookies for crunching."

"No more food. You've had enough."

"No ice cream? What's wrong with you?"

"You can barely breathe."

"I'm not going to deprive myself of ice cream.
If I do, I'll get upset and eat the whole carton
when I wake up in the middle of the night."

"Deprive yourself? You are far
from depriving yourself.
You weigh more than 200 pounds
and it didn't happen
because you didn't eat food."

"But in this very moment when I salivate
for ice cream, every cell of my body is waiting
for the reward it deserves after such a tough day.
If I don't give it pleasure, it would be as if I
abandoned my whole body, and that could be fatal."

"You know better than I that the fatality can
happen if you keep eating and getting bigger.
It was a doctor who told you that you're pre-diabetic
and it's only a matter of time before you get sick."

"I'm already sick. When I have to eat less
I feel as if the whole world is spinning,

and I feel there's a lump in my throat—a tightness that chokes me."

"I don't know how to talk to you anymore.
All I know is that disaster is coming."

*"Well, it will come anyway, so why not relax
and enjoy the moments that are left?"*

"You really don't care whether you live or die?"

*"Come on. Of course I do but I don't want to
live as if I was walking on sharp nails either."*

"Then why can't you just be satisfied with what is enough?"

"Enough? Who knows what enough is? You?"

"Well, there must be a way to find out.
I'm sure that you eat enough to get bigger,
so maybe you can find enough to get smaller."

*"I didn't know that you were a trickster.
Enough to get bigger is not the same
as enough to get smaller. Again you want
me to starve my body and you know I'll never do it."*

"And then what will happen?"

"We'll have fun until we drop."

"I don't want that kind of fun. I want fun that
is constructive and makes us better."

*"You have become naive, too.
Do you really believe that you can
deprive yourself by eating less
and that you can actually enjoy it?"*

"I not only believe that it is possible.
I know it is possible.
It is the feeling I have in my whole body."

*"So you are a dreamer after all.
Let's have some ice cream."*

"In three hours. In three hours."

IV. Hesitator:

"I feel so full. This ice cream looks
very tempting but I've had enough for today.
Maybe I'll have some tomorrow."

*"There must be some room left
just for a scoop of ice cream?"*

"You're right—it looks delicious
but I feel tired and tomorrow will be a tough day
so I'd better go to bed."

"Just one scoop."

"Tomorrow. Tomorrow."

V. Master:

"I feel so full. I'd better go for a long
walk to help me digest all this food.
Today I'll walk all around the park. It's almost
two hours of a pleasant walk.
It'll be enough time for me to relax
and get ready for a nice long sleep."

MOVIE THEATER

Scenario 11. Jen is in the movie theater, looking forward to seeing the movie with her favorite actress, standing in the line to buy snacks.

I. Fatalist:

*"I love going to movies and there isn't
anything better than an American movie theater.
I can sit in my comfortable seat
enjoying the film and the food.
This movie is more than two hours long
so I'm sure I'll get very hungry.
I'll get a large popcorn and large soda
with free refills for both.
It'll be a fantastic."*

II. Disbeliever:

*"I love going to movies and there isn't
anything better than an American movie theater.
I can sit in my comfortable seat
enjoying the film and the food.
This movie is more than two hours long
so I'm sure I'll get very hungry.
I'll get a large popcorn and large soda
with free refills for both.*

It'll be a fantastic."

"Refill? Don't you think
it's too tempting to overeat that way?
You just had a large latte with almond milk—
probably hundreds of calories."

*"But it's a movie night, and with
my favorite actress. What could be
a bigger reason to celebrate?"*

"You can have some apples and water.
It's healthier and much cheaper, too."

"Sorry, but apples are not romantic."

"But you are alone."

*"You never know. There could be a man
waiting for me and I'm sure he won't eat apples."*

"What if ..."

"Enough. I'm happy and I won't ruin it."

III. Debater:

*"I love going to movies and there isn't
anything better than an American movie theater.*

128

I can sit in my comfortable seat
enjoying the film and the food.
This movie is more than two hours long
so I'm sure I'll get very hungry.
I'll get a large popcorn and large soda
with free refills for both.
It'll be a fantastic."

"Do you think it's a pleasure to watch you eating
popcorn and hear you slurping soda for two hours?"

"Do you think it's a pleasure when you drag me
to the other side of the city to an art museum
to look at paintings of long dead artists?
At least I take you to the movie so you can
get excited and make your depressing face happy."

"You're comparing artists to entertainers?
I've never thought that you go to movies
to become happy for even one moment.
I take you to museums so you can find happiness forever."

"Happiness forever? I didn't know
you bought into that flashy language.
Let's have some popcorn and soda and
actually enjoy being present."

"That's what you're best at—being present
without any vision of tomorrow."

*"I'd rather be happy and poor
than rich and unhappy."*

"What if it's possible to be both?"

*"Dream on, dream on.
Have you ever seen any of your friends
happy to be working fourteen hours a day?"*

"No, but I saw movies about people like that."

"So you're a wishful thinker after all."

"No, I'm going to create this person,
and you will enjoy it, too."

IV. Hesitator:

"It's always difficult to order any food
in the movie theater and I cannot bring my own.
There is definitely nothing healthy to eat, so
I'll have some green tea."

*"Just take a deep breath.
Do you smell the wonderful aroma
of popcorn? How about just a small box?
It's fresh and must be good for the body
in small quantities, and look around—
everyone has a box of popcorn and a soda."*

"You can't imagine how happy it makes me
that I don't do what everyone else does.
Green tea will be soothing."

V. Master:

"This movie theater is great.
It's so large that I don't have to smell
all the popcorn and I can go straight
to my seat and watch my movie."

MIDDLE-OF-THE-NIGHT HUNGER

Scenario 12. It is 2 am. Jen wakes up feeling hungry.

I. Fatalist:

*"It's great that I bought some chocolate bars yesterday.
I will go downstairs and eat some."*

II. Disbeliever:

*"It's great that I bought some chocolate bars yesterday.
I will go downstairs and eat some."*

"Maybe you can relax and the hunger will go away.
You can always have some after breakfast."

*"I can't stop thinking about chocolate melting in my mouth.
If I don't eat it, I will be awake the whole night."*

"I'm sure you will eventually fall asleep.
Just stay in bed for another fifteen minutes."

*"Why would I try to avoid eating chocolate?
Life without it is not worth living."*

III. Debater:

*"It's great that I bought some chocolate bars yesterday.
I will go downstairs and eat some."*

"Don't even think about doing that."

"Why not? I'm hungry."

"Hungry? Just four hours ago you had
a three-course dinner with a steak, mashed potatoes,
and an enormous piece of cheesecake."

*"That doesn't change the fact that my stomach is empty
and I am starving."*

"The more you eat, the more hungry you become.
You used to sleep through the night but this year
you often wake up at night
and make the trip downstairs to the kitchen."

*"Don't exaggerate. I don't even remember when
I last woke up at night and ate anything."*

"Really? Let me refresh your memory.
Yesterday you woke up at 3 am and ate a whole bag of walnuts."

"Oh. I completely forgot about that."

"Three days ago you woke up at 1 am and ate
a whole hazelnut chocolate bar."

*"All right. All right. It's just that I have this fear that
I will die if I don't eat when I'm hungry."*

"Then try to relax, and maybe you can fall asleep."

*"I would but I don't understand why I can't go downstairs.
It's just some chocolate and it relaxes me.
And you know, I always fall asleep after eating it."*

"I guess I need to remind you what you say in the morning
after your little escapade to the kitchen."

"What? That I love chocolate or nuts?"

"What about this—
I messed up again. I lost it. What is wrong with me?
I will never lose weight."

"Everybody has moments of weakness. I'm no exception."

"No, but you want to be healthy and you are already pre-diabetic.
If you keep losing your grip on this
you will be fulfilling the famous advertising slogan
'death by chocolate.'"

"I knew you were melodramatic.
Many overweight people live a long and happy life."

"Many but not most. Do you really want to risk your life?"

"Well, of course I don't, but there must be compromise.
Life is not about perfection."

"Can you pick up a book and read?
I'm sure it will help you relax."

"I'm not in the mood to read right now,
but I will read tomorrow. Compromise?"

"Tomorrow. I've heard that before."

IV. Hesitator:

"I'm so glad I'm hungry.
I must be eating less than I need.
Maybe, after all, I will lose all this
unnecessary fat that I've accumulated over the years."

"But there is some chocolate in the kitchen
and you always relax after having some.

I'm sure it wouldn't hurt you, since
you are doing so well on this diet."

"I will have some at breakfast.
I love feeling lighter
and I'm so happy I can wait."

V. Master:

"I'm hungry. That is great news.
There must still be a thousand
food bars turned into fat
spreading all over my body.
I still feel like a walking Safeway.
Go and find some bars."

Part II
Practice Personalizing the Book's 12 Scenarios

What Would the Master within Me Say?
What Would the Fatalist within Me Say?

Make the Master's voice the last in the Debate.

THE SCALE

Scenario 1. You are standing on the scale, which is showing a three-pound gain from the day before.

Fatalist:

F _____

Disbeliever:

F _____

M_____

F _____

Debater:

F _____

M_____

F _____

M_____

F _____

M_____

Hesitator:

F _____

M_____

F _____

Master:

F _____

BREAKFAST

Scenario 2. It is 7 am. You are staring at a piece of bread with a thin layer of almond butter on top of it. Your nutritionist told you the day before to consume no more than 150 calories for breakfast, in order to lose 45 pounds of fat in seven months.

Fatalist:

F _____

Disbeliever:

F _____
M_____
F _____

Debater:

F _____
M_____
F _____
M_____
F _____
M_____

Hesitator:

F _____
M_____
F _____

Master:

F _____

LUNCH

Scenario 3. You are sitting with three friends at a table in a restaurant, reading the menu.
Your friend Angela has always had a perfect figure. June is 20-30 pounds overweight and has always struggled with losing weight. Monica, who is about 100 pounds overweight, has never seemed to care about her weight problem.

Fatalist:

F _____

Disbeliever:

F _____

M_____

F _____

Debater:

F _____

M_____

F _____

M_____

F _____

M_____

Hesitator:

F _____

M_____

F _____

Master:

F _____

DOCTOR'S OFFICE

Scenario 4. Your doctor tells you: "You are already pre-diabetic. With your family history, if you don't lose at least 25 pounds in a hurry, you could become diabetic within six months."

Fatalist:

F _____

Disbeliever:

F _____

M_____

F _____

Debater:

F _____

M_____

F _____

M_____

F _____

M_____

Hesitator:

F _____

M_____

F _____

Master:

F _____

INSIDE THE GROCERY STORE

Scenario 5. You have walked into the store from the side where fruits and vegetables are displayed.

Fatalist:

F _____

Disbeliever:

F _____

M_____

F _____

Debater:

F _____

M_____

F _____

M_____

F _____

M_____

Hesitator:

F _____

M_____

F _____

Master:

F _____

THE LAST 10 POUNDS

Scenario 6. You are reading a chart that shows no weight loss during the past two years, even though you have tried everything you can think of to achieve your weight-loss goal.

Fatalist:

F _____

Disbeliever:

F _____

M_____

F _____

Debater:

F _____

M_____

F _____

M_____

F _____

M_____

Hesitator:

F _____

M_____

F _____

Master:

F _____

TASTING FOOD

Scenario 7. You have been stopped in the grocery store by a food company representative to taste a new product sample. Looking at it, you don't know what it is.

Fatalist:

F _____

Disbeliever:

F _____
M_____
F _____

Debater:

F _____
M_____
F _____
M_____
F _____
M_____

Hesitator:

F _____
M_____
F _____

Master:

F _____

PREPARING A DINNER

Scenario 8. You are preparing a dinner for your friends, Anna and Fred. Fred is gluten intolerant.

Fatalist:

F _____

Disbeliever:

F _____

M_____

F _____

Debater:

F _____

M_____

F _____

M_____

F _____

M_____

Hesitator:

F _____

M_____

F _____

Master:

F _____

"ALL YOU CAN EAT"

Scenario 9. You are on a ski vacation. You are in the restaurant together with your spouse and two children. You sit down at a table with other three couples and their children. There are 16 of you altogether.
The waiter presents the options: "Every Saturday, we have a special dinner, which you can order from the menu. Or you can select the all-you-can-eat buffet."

Fatalist:

F _____

Disbeliever:

F _____

M_____

F _____

Debater:

F _____

M_____

F _____

M_____

F _____

M_____

Hesitator:

F _____

M_____

F _____

Master:

F _____

AFTER DINNER

Scenario 10. It is 7 pm. Finishing dinner, you have a strong urge for something sweet.

Fatalist:

F _____

Disbeliever:

F _____

M_____

F _____

Debater:

F _____

M_____

F _____

M_____

F _____

M_____

Hesitator:

F _____

M_____

F _____

Master:

F _____

MOVIE THEATER

Scenario 11. You are in the movie theater, looking forward to seeing the movie with your favorite actress, standing in the line to buy snacks.

Fatalist:

F _____

Disbeliever:

F _____

M_____

F _____

Debater:

F _____

M_____

F _____

M_____

F _____

M_____

Hesitator:

F _____

M_____

F _____

Master:

F _____

MIDDLE-OF-THE NIGHT HUNGER

Scenario 12. You wake up feeling hungry at 2 am.

Fatalist:

F _____

Disbeliever:

F _____
M_____
F _____

Debater:

F _____
M_____
F _____
M_____
F _____
M_____

Hesitator:

F _____
M_____
F _____

Master:

F _____

Part III
Practice Writing Your Own Scenarios

Before writing out the dialogues, describe the basic nature of the situation.

Scenario _____
_____
_____

Fatalist:

F _____

Disbeliever:

F _____
M_____
F _____

Debater:

F _____
M_____
F _____
M_____
F _____
M_____

Hesitator:

F _____
M_____
F _____

Master:

F _____

Scenario _____

_____

_____

Fatalist:

F _____

Disbeliever:

F _____

M_____

F _____

Debater:

F _____

M_____

F _____

M_____

F _____

M_____

Hesitator:

F _____

M_____

F _____

Master:

F _____

Scenario _____
_____
_____

Fatalist:
F _____

Disbeliever:
F _____
M_____
F _____

Debater:
F _____
M_____
F _____
M_____
F _____
M_____

Hesitator:
F _____
M_____
F _____

Master:
F _____

Scenario _____

_____

_____

Fatalist:

F _____

Disbeliever:

F _____

M_____

F _____

Debater:

F _____

M_____

F _____

M_____

F _____

M_____

Hesitator:

F _____

M_____

F _____

Master:

F _____

Scenario _____

_____

_____

Fatalist:

F _____

Disbeliever:

F _____

M_____

F _____

Debater:

F _____

M_____

F _____

M_____

F _____

M_____

Hesitator:

F _____

M_____

F _____

Master:

F _____

Scenario _____

_____

_____

Fatalist:
F _____

Disbeliever:
F _____
M_____
F _____

Debater:
F _____
M_____
F _____
M_____
F _____
M_____

Hesitator:
F _____
M_____
F _____

Master:
F _____

Scenario _____

_____

_____

Fatalist:

F _____

Disbeliever:

F _____

M_____

F _____

Debater:

F _____

M_____

F _____

M_____

F _____

M_____

Hesitator:

F _____

M_____

F _____

Master:

F _____

Scenario _____

_____

_____

Fatalist:

F _____

Disbeliever:

F _____

M_____

F _____

Debater:

F _____

M_____

F _____

M_____

F _____

M_____

Hesitator:

F _____

M_____

F _____

Master:

F _____

Scenario _____

_____

_____

Fatalist:

F _____

Disbeliever:

F _____

M_____

F _____

Debater:

F _____

M_____

F _____

M_____

F _____

M_____

Hesitator:

F _____

M_____

F _____

Master:

F _____

Scenario _____

_____

_____

Fatalist:

F _____

Disbeliever:

F _____

M_____

F _____

Debater:

F _____

M_____

F _____

M_____

F _____

M_____

Hesitator:

F _____

M_____

F _____

Master:

F _____

Scenario _____

_____

_____

Fatalist:

F _____

Disbeliever:

F _____

M_____

F _____

Debater:

F _____

M_____

F _____

M_____

F _____

M_____

Hesitator:

F _____

M_____

F _____

Master:

F _____

Scenario _____

_____

_____

Fatalist:

F _____

Disbeliever:

F _____

M_____

F _____

Debater:

F _____

M_____

F _____

M_____

F _____

M_____

Hesitator:

F _____

M_____

F _____

Master:

F _____

Please don't be discouraged if you fail in any situation. Begin by clearly identifying it. Then write out the five-level dialogue, using the formula provided in the templates above. Pinpoint the level at which you currently find yourself. Practice "importing" the message from level five into your real-life scenario (self conditioning), until the voice of the Master within you triumphs.

For information on *The Happy Body* Program, including possible updates relating to The Way of Conscious Eating, please visit TheHappyBody.com.

You are always welcome to share your personal success story with the author, via Jerzy@TheHappyBody.com.

Watch your thoughts; they become words.
Watch your words; they become actions.
Watch your actions; they become habit.
Watch your habits; they become character.
Watch your character; it becomes your destiny.

—Lao Tzu

CONTRARY CONVICTIONS	
The Fatalist	**The Master**
It's too hard.	I know it's hard but I want the benefits.
It's impossible.	It's possible.
I love food too much to eat less.	I love good health enough to eat less.
I'm too old to change.	It's never too late to change.
It's not normal at my age to be thin.	Being trim at any age is healthier.
I'm already old.	I can become more youthful.
I'll die if I eat so little.	Eating appropriately will extend my life.
I won't get enough nutrition.	I eat only nutritious food.
I still don't believe it's possible.	I'll try it and see.
I would starve myself.	If I lose too much weight, I can eat more.
I'm heavier because I'm on my period.	My period is no excuse for gaining weight.
It's not fun to always control oneself.	I can have fun while controlling myself.
Only poor people cook these days.	Intelligent people cook for themselves.
Being fat is normal.	Being trim is normal for healthy people.
Life is short, so enjoy it while you can.	I refuse to shorten my life.
I don't trust science.	I acknowledge reality.
I trust my appetite.	I trust my knowledge.

I don't care about others.	My actions take others into account.
I'll party until I drop.	I'll have fun in a way that's good for me.
I can't get by eating so little.	I will eat only as much as I need to.
I won't struggle with what's difficult.	I won't avoid what's difficult.
I've hit a plateau.	I plan my plateaus.
Nothing works.	Everything works.
I love to get things for free.	I prefer to earn what I get.
Protecting my health is a waste of time.	Protecting my health saves time.
Constant planning is annoying.	Planning is liberating.
I'll do it tomorrow.	I'll do it today.
I hate the clock.	The clock is my friend.
I don't like to do boring things.	Anything can be interesting.
I prefer to live in a fantasy.	I prefer to have both feet on the ground.
People irritate me.	People help me give meaning to my life.
I need more.	I only need enough.
I can't lose weight no matter what I do.	There are many options for losing weight.
I live for the moment.	I live for the long term.
I wish I could buy fitness.	I'm happy I can achieve fitness for myself.
Getting older is depressing.	Life can be enjoyable at any age.
"Enough" is never enough.	"Enough" is always enough.
I'll stop eating when I feel satisfied.	I'll stop eating when I've had enough.
I'll be happy to have finished my work.	I'm happy to be working.
I don't believe in criticizing my friends.	A true friend is always honest.
I want others to inspire me.	I love to inspire myself.
Diets don't work.	Every diet works.
I complain when something is wrong.	I fix what is wrong.
I hope I'll eat less.	I will eat less.
I offer advice to anyone about anything.	I only advise in my area of expertise.

Eating is everything.	Living is everything.
I wish my excess fat would disappear.	I'm responsible for reducing my excess fat.
I blame food companies for my obesity.	I tune out unhealthy advertising.
I fear being hungry.	I fear overeating.
Packaged foods are the most appealing.	Fresh produce is the best kind of food.
I'm not interested in how foods are made.	I want to know how my food is produced.
I want a pill to suppress my appetite.	I decide what goes in my mouth and when.
I'm not smart enough.	I have what it takes.
I could never be like that.	I can be whatever I want to be.
I don't deserve that.	I am as worthy as anyone else is.
"Life is short: eat dessert first."	Life is long: eat healthy food first.
I don't have time.	I always have time for what's important.
I don't have the energy for change.	I'll get stronger, so I'll have more energy.
I was born this way.	I focus on becoming better.
I can't fight my genes.	I can fit into my jeans.
Actors and models are paid to be thin.	Being fit and trim will increase my options.
You can't fight destiny.	I create my own destiny.
"The devil made me do it."	I can be my own angel.
I can't change my environment.	I choose how I respond to my environment.
ADD YOUR OWN PAIRS	

NOTES

ABOUT THE AUTHOR

Jerzy Gregorek immigrated to the United States together with his wife, Aniela, from Poland in 1986, as political refugees during the Solidarity Movement. An accomplished athlete, he subsequently won four World Weightlifting Championships and established one world record. In 2000, Jerzy and Aniela founded UCLA's weightlifting team, becoming its head coaches. As co-creator of *The Happy Body* Program, Jerzy has been mentoring people for more than 30 years, helping them attain a happy and healthy lifestyle.

In 1998, Jerzy earned an MFA in writing from the Vermont College of Fine Arts. His poems and translations have appeared in numerous publications, including *The American Poetry Review*. His poem "Family Tree" was the winner of *Amelia* magazine's Charles William Duke Longpoem Award in 1998.

In 2002, the National Endowment for the Arts awarded Jerzy a literature fellowship to support the translation from Polish into English of selected poems by Maurycy Szymel. This culminated in the publication in 2013 of *The Shy Hand of a Jew* by Cross-Cultural Communications, which the following year published a collection of Jerzy's own poetry, entitled *Sacred and Scared*. *A Healthy Mirror for Change: Nourishing an Appetite for Losing Weight*, another volume of poetry, was also published in 2014.

This latest book harnesses the power of the discovery of a series of internal dialogues, to help readers achieve important goals in the realm of health and fitness. This is accomplished first by understanding the tension and interplay between the voices of what are termed the

Fatalist and the Master within all of us. Readers are then invited to first extend these dialogues into their own lives—and subsequently to articulate other key scenarios in their lives that are playing themselves out along similar lines. Ultimately, by importing the critical message into these various scenarios, you enable the voice of the Master within you to triumph.

Jerzy lives with his wife and their daughter in Woodside, California.